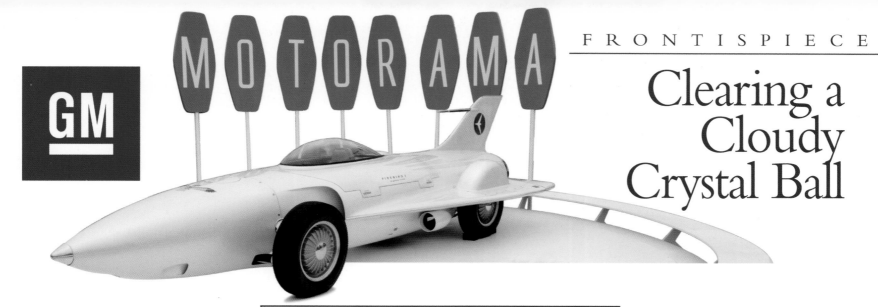

Clearing a Cloudy Crystal Ball

General Motors was once famous for sharing visions of the future with the Motorama traveling road show and the associated exciting concept cars on display. Following World War II, GM fed "car hungry" consumers exciting designs to tempt a purchase.

In the pre-Japanese and European "auto invasion" days, the Motorama Miracle was a master marketing stroke that provided quick feedback from consumers and kept assembly lines busy and dealer showrooms full.

Although the last official Motorama concluded in 1961, the concept cars and restored GM Futurliner are still compelling draws at concours events. The models comprise a nostalgic look at the past, looking to the future, as was demonstrated at Pebble Beach in 2008.

However, the rigors of the 21st century haven't been kind to the 100-year-old giant as it struggles to survive, and it would seem that the light of the GM crystal ball has dimmed significantly. Toyota recently outsold any of the Big Three, displacing GM from the number-one international sales position; GM's cash burn-through is akin to a Bessemer steel furnace, and its "retro designs" (but don't call them that), such as

"Trees sent Joyce Kilmer, but nothing quite sends most Americans like the smell of a new-car interior and the soul-satisfying sound of shutting a new-car door. There are few among us who don't find that sound as exciting as any bar of music … call it what you want, or call for the psychiatrist, but it's a powerful fact of American life."

Malcom Forbes

the GTO reintroduction and the SSR, failed to ignite excitement and sales worthy of line continuance.

So now what? Automotive business restructuring and realigning are nothing new. Author and historian Beverly Rae Kimes estimated that there have been more than 3,000 automobile companies formed in this country alone, with only three (some would argue 2.5) remaining. There is no argument concerning the impact of the automotive industry on our overall economy, and there is no desire to see any of the three fail. Yet, the intense pressure of the economy, international competition and energy issues demand an energetic and fundamental change. As Charles F.

Kettering observed, "The world hates change, yet it is the only thing that has brought progress."

If GM is to change, and surely it must, we would hope for a change for the better, for an automotive industry that recognizes that cars, like their human drivers, are lasting longer, living better, and expecting more from everything in their lives, especially the cars they drive.

History has shown us that no person and no company can accurately and consistently predict the future. That doesn't mean we stop introducing new design ideas. In fact, they're needed even more. In this time of transformation, we need reactive companies that restructure to cope more efficiently with change, to rethink, reinvent and reinvigorate. I suggest less "bean counting" and more customer contact. The crystal ball works well only with constant polishing from design and innovative engineering. And, oh yes, did I mention honest customer feedback?

Drive in Peace,

Gerry Durnell

Gerry Durnell
Editor & Publisher

1

Automobile Quarterly

The Connoisseur's Publication of Motoring
– Today, Yesterday, and Tomorrow –

GERRY DURNELL
Editor & Publisher

KAYE BOWLES-DURNELL
Associate Publisher

JOHN C. DURNELL
Chief Operations Officer, Technical Editor

TRACY POWELL
Managing Editor

LARRY CRANE
West Coast Editor

JOHN EVANS
Chief Financial Officer

DAN BULLEIT
Art Director

ROD HOTTLE
Administrative Assistant

ROBIN JEFFERS
Customer Service

L. SCOTT BAILEY
Founding Editor and Publisher

Contributing Photographers
CAM HUTCHINS
NED LAWLER, ANDREW MORT
WEST PETERSON, DENIS TANNEY
ARD OP DE WEEGH

Contributing Writers
LEIGH DORRINGTON
PETER HILDEBRANDT
NED LAWLER, KARL LUDVIGSEN
NORM MORT, BARRY PATCHETT
WEST PETERSON, BILL ROTHERMEL
ARNOUD & ARD OP DE WEEGH

www.autoquarterly.com

ISBN 1-59613-060-1

(978-1-59613-060-9)

Printed in Korea

Contents

VOLUME 48, NUMBER 4 • FOURTH QUARTER 2008

Ray Harroun in the 1911 race-winning Marmon, surrounded by multiple-500 winners A.J. Foyt, Bobby Unser, Al Unser Sr., Bill Vukovich, Wilbur Shaw, Johnny Rutherford, Louis Meyer, Tommy Milton, Gordon Johncock, Mauri Rose, Rick Mears and Roger Ward.

Cover: Art by Bernie Fuchs

First in a series to commemorate the 75th anniversary of the Indianapolis 500, 1991.

CAMORADI BIRDCAGE
Once in a Lifetime

Synchronicity is defined as a coincidence of events that seem related but are not obviously caused by one another. What else would explain two uncrowned world champions sharing a car the constructor refused to race, winning one of the most legendary international sports-car races in history, and driving for an unknown team owner? Stirling Moss and Dan Gurney won the 1,000-km sports-car race at the Nürburgring in 1960, co-driving a Tipo 61 "Birdcage" Maserati entered by the American CAMORADI team. That much is history. The story is how it came to be.

BY LEIGH DORRINGTON

STIRLING MOSS

Moss was more than the greatest driver of his generation, although he was most certainly that. Now Sir Stirling Moss, he has lived for nearly half a century as this is written, graciously accepting the title of "The Champion Without a Crown." In 1960, he was universally regarded as the best driver in the world.

Moss began racing in the postwar 500cc formula against other newcomers, including Mike Hawthorn and Peter Collins, both of whom became among his closest friends and competitors. Moss gained early wins with a Cooper, including a victory in the Formula Three race at Goodwood in September 1948 that was the first race ever contested at the now-hallowed Goodwood circuit.

Two major milestones occurred for Moss in 1950. The first was a contract to drive an HWM in formula races. The second was his first international victory in sports cars, at Dunrod in Ireland in a Jaguar XK120.

By 1951, Moss' name was on everyone's lips. He continued to race in Formula Two with HWM. The Swiss Grand Prix in May against Formula One machines marked his first World Championship race, where he was competitive with the larger Ferraris, Alfa Romeos and Talbot-Lagos before running out of fuel on the last lap. He also undertook a full season in Formula Three, driving a new Norton-powered Keift. In the first race of the season, at the difficult Nürburgring, he broke the lap record by 40 seconds.

He also was signed as a driver for Jaguar's attempt at overall victory at Le Mans with the new C-Type. The 22-year-old Moss set fastest lap and was leading the race when the failure of an oil fitting took him out

of contention; the contest was won by teammates Peter Walker and Peter Whitehead in another C-Type.

Perhaps the most important development in motorsports in 1951 was one that didn't happen. Enzo Ferrari watched Moss as closely as anyone and telegrammed that Moss would be welcome at Ferrari in 1952. In preparation, Moss was offered a drive in a 2.5-liter Ferrari for the Bari Grand Prix in September 1951. When he arrived on the Adriatic coast to be fitted to the car, however, Moss was brusquely informed by the Ferrari mechanics that the car was for Piero Taruffi. This apparent slight would propel Moss's career for the next decade.

Throughout his career, Moss showed a resolute commitment to succeed in British automobiles. During 1952 and 1953, he raced a confounding range of British machines with a frustrating lack of success. This lack of success in British cars was all the more frustrating because Mike Hawthorn had started to make a name for himself with Ferrari in 1953.

It was clear that something different would be needed – quickly. Alfred Moss and manager Ken Gregory contacted Mercedes-Benz's legendary team manager Alfred Neubauer, who was known to be returning to grand prix racing. Neubauer replied that although he had yet to see Moss race in a competitive grand prix machine, he would continue to keep an eye on him. The only other option for a competitive grand prix car, then, was Maserati.

Alfred Moss and Gregory purchased a Maserati 250F (s/n2508) from the factory for Stirling to drive in the 1954 grand prix season. Moss scored his first World Championship points with the privately entered Maserati, painted British racing green, at the Belgian Grand Prix at Spa in June 1954, as well as four non-championship Formula One races in the UK.

In December 1954, Moss had a private test with the Mercedes W196 grand prix car at Hockenheim in Germany. He was signed to race for Mercedes-Benz in 1955 in both Formula One and sports cars, teamed with Mercedes' 1954 World Champion Juan Fangio.

It was a glory season. Moss started the sports-car season with a historic win in the first race of the sea-

Moss won four races in 1953 in the Formula Three Keift-Norton. The car's far forward driving position and adjustable suspension gave significant advantages, according to Moss.

established for the racing program had been accomplished and the team would be retired. Moss tested the three British Formula One cars – BRM, Connaught and Vanwall – at Silverstone but was unconvinced of their reliability. Moss found himself back with Maserati, this time as the lead works driver, where he again finished second in the World Championship to Fangio in a Ferrari.

Moss raced with the British Vanwall team in 1957 and won three of the six World Championship Formula One races, but finished second yet again to Fangio, who had returned to Maserati, where he won his fifth world championship. He finished second in the championship in 1958 to Mike Hawthorn, driving for Ferrari, by just one point.

Combined with Fangio's retirement during the 1958 season, surely 1959 would be Stirling Moss' year. But it was not to be – again – when Moss dropped to third in the World Championship in a privately entered Rob Walker Cooper.

Moss also drove an Aston Martin DBR1 sports car for the 1959 season. At the 1,000-km race at the Nürburgring, he enjoyed one of the best races of his life. Leading from the start, he broke his own lap record 16 times in his first driving stint and turned the car over to his co-driver Jack Fairman with a 6:30 lead. Fairman was forced off the track on the 23rd lap and

son, teamed with journalist Denis Jenkinson, at the Mille Miglia, before adding other dominating wins in the 300SLR sports car at the Nürburgring, Dunrod and the Targa Florio.

Fangio and Moss frequently ran first and second throughout the 1955 Formula One season, and Moss' first Formula One victory came with Mercedes in 1955. In spite of his success in sports cars, this victory must have been the highlight of the year, coming at the British Grand Prix at Aintree before his home crowd and leading a Mercedes-Benz 1-2-3-4 finish. Silver-haired Pierro Taruffi drove the fourth-place Mercedes. Fangio repeated as World Champion, and Moss finished second in the championship.

But the glory was short lived. At the end of the 1955 season, Mercedes-Benz announced that the goals

Top left: Stirling Moss won the 1954 12 Hours of Sebring in March with Bill Lloyd in an OSCA entered by Briggs Cunningham, and in June scored his first Formula One World Championship points with his privately-entered Maserati 250F. Above: Moss often carried the lucky number 7 early in his career, here in the C-Type Jaguar in 1951.

returned to the pits 1:10 behind the new leader. "Moss drove like a man possessed in what is now a legendary drive," wrote Pierre Menard and Jacques Vassal in their excellent biography *Stirling Moss, The Champion Without a Crown*. "On lap 29 he had got the lead back from the Ferraris and on lap 33 he had extended it to two minutes."

"It was the kind of race I like best," Moss said later. "A green and solitary Aston against the entire team of red factory Ferraris." How different things would be just a year later.

Dan Gurney

Dan Gurney was the up-and-coming man in international racing in 1960. He had not even started his first sports-car race in 1955 when Moss was enjoying his glory season with Mercedes-Benz. He had raced in informal drag races and at the Bonneville Salt Flats. Later he drove endless laps in a Porsche through an unfinished Southern California housing development and sneaked into the Riverside racecourse before it was completed. His first road race was in a well-used Triumph TR-2 at Torrey Pines, Calif., in October 1955. He entered the Triumph again in the next race at Palm Springs, without noticeable results in either.

However, Gurney was noticed by everyone present at Riverside just two years later. He drove an ill-handling 4.9-liter Ferrari owned by Frank Arciero and finished second to Carroll Shelby. Historian Karl Ludvigsen described how "few drivers have made more of a reputation by finishing second." Gurney had competed in only 12 sports-car races prior to Riverside.

Other top rides came his way, including drives in a Maserati 450S and Ferrari 250GTs. He drove a tiny French DB coupe at Sebring in 1958, but his best result was a brief four laps of practice at Sebring in a Ferrari 250GT, observed by Luigi Chinetti, who won the 1949 24 Hours of Le Mans in a Ferrari and was Ferrari's importer in the United States. Chinetti was also Ferrari's official entrant in U.S. races with his leg-endary North American Racing Team (NART).

Chinetti offered an invitation to drive for NART at Le Mans in 1958. The call couldn't have come at a better time, as Gurney found himself balanced on a knife's edge between his desire to become a professional racing driver and his need to provide for his family. The Ferraris he entered at both Le Mans and the Reims 12-hour race were crashed by codrivers, but Gurney remained in Europe.

Photojournalist Bernard Cahier introduced Gurney to the private Scuderia Centro Sud team which entered him in a 1.5-liter OSCA at the Nürburgring, a track he

Some of Dan Gurney's earliest successes came in the Arciero Brothers 4.9-liter Ferrari, beating top California drivers including Carroll Shelby, Chuck Daigh, Billy Kraus and Max Balchowsky.

had never seen, where he finished seventh. "I didn't even see 'em after the race started," Ludvigsen quoted Gurney as saying. "But I kept my head down and was trying to drive the circuit. Every little experience you could get in those days at that place was really worth it. They said I had driven an OSCA nearly 20 seconds a lap quicker than anybody else had ever done."

In November 1958, Gurney was invited to test for Ferrari at the recommendation of Chinetti and American Phil Hill. Gurney was offered three sports-car starts for Ferrari in 1959, including Sebring, the Targa Florio and the Nürburgring. He was also given a test in a Ferrari

Formula One car at Monza in June 1959. The test was successful, and he started his first Formula One grand prix at Reims on July 5, 1959, in a V6 Ferrari Dino. Gurney was chosen to finish the grand prix season teamed with Tony Brooks and Hill.

He answered with a second-place finish in his first race at Avus, followed by a third and a fourth. The British publication *Autosport* declared, "Dan Gurney is undoubtedly the find of the season … the young American has proved that he can hold his own with the best European drivers."

Despite this brilliant debut, however, Ferrari remained committed to a front-engine GP car for 1960. This was in spite of the success of new rear-engine designs from Cooper, including the car that won the 1959 World Championship for Australian Jack Brabham. "I had a front-row seat for the design contest," Ludvigsen quoted Gurney as saying later. "I could see that an engine in the rear, behind the driver, was the way to go." After just nine races with Ferrari, in sports cars and Formula One, Gurney signed with BRM for the 1960 grand prix season.

MASERATI TIPO 60/61 "BIRDCAGE"

ive Maserati brothers joined the automobile industry *(Automobile Quarterly, Vol. 5 No. 3)*. Carlo, Bindo, Alfieri, Ettore and Ernesto Maserati all found themselves involved with early Italian automakers, developing, testing – and sometimes racing – F.I.A.T., Bianchi, Isotta-Fraschini and Diatto, before the first car to carry the Maserati name, the Tipo 26, was designed and constructed in 1926. The trident carried by the statue of Neptune in the main square of Bologna, where the car was built, was adopted as the Maserati symbol.

The Tipo 26 was immediately successful, winning its class in the car's first race, the 1926 Targa Florio, driven by Alfieri with riding mechanic Guerrino Bertocchi, who would remain with Maserati for more than 50 years. Other successful Maserati designs followed.

Maserati enjoyed spectacular prewar racing success, but the marque did not share the commercial success of Bugatti or Alfa Romeo for the simple reason that

Ing. Alfieri would have preferred to build a more modern monocoque chassis, but the resources were not available to him. The "birdcage" frame was the ultimate development of the successful 250F "piccolo" GP design.

Maserati only built racing cars. By 1937, the loss of two of the brothers and the effects of the Great Depression led the surviving brothers to sell the company, Officine Alfieri Maserati, to the Orsi industrial family of Modena. Bindo, Ettore and Ernesto agreed to contracts that bound them to Orsi from 1937-1947 and operations moved to Modena.

Luigi Villoresi won the first postwar grand prix at Nice on April 22, 1946, in a Maserati 4CL based on a prewar design. However, at the end of their 10-year agreement with Orsi, the Maserati brothers departed with little fanfare, returned to Bologna and founded a new auto company, Officine Specialzate Costruzione Automobili Fratelli Maserati (OSCA). Maserati foundered without the design leadership and experience of the brothers.

It was an all-new car designed for the 1954 2.5-liter Formula One series, the immortal 250F, that would return Maserati to greatness. Of all the great grand prix cars of the 1950s, none achieved more enduring success than the Maserati 250F. Fangio won the first two races of the 1954 Formula One season in a 250F before departing to join Mercedes-Benz. Moss gained his first real success in Formula One in a privately owned 250F. Returning to Maserati in 1956 after Mercedes retired from racing, Moss won two World Championship grands prix and five nonchampionship events on 250Fs. Fangio returned to Maserati in 1957 and won his fifth World Championship. Privately entered 250Fs filled grand prix grids of the 2.5-liter era from 1954 through 1960.

Maserati also excelled in sports-car racing in 1956 and 1957 with the 300S and the 450S, taking the World Sports Car Championship to the final race of the season only to lose to Ferrari each time. In 1957, Maserati lost more than the championship.

With a chance to win the championship at the final

Above: Unusual tubular construction is fully visible in the Birdcage's cockpit. Below: Gurney dives out of the car and Moss prepares to enter, exhibiting a frenetic level of activity trying to bring the Birdcage up to speed. The BP mechanics in the next pit exhibit detachment.

1957 race in Caracas, Venezuela, the entire team of four factory-entered Maseratis and one privately entered car all crashed – two into each other – or dropped out of the race. In addition to the loss of the championship, Maserati lost the expected income from selling the cars at the end of the season. In addition to the heavy cost of supporting the Formula One team, Maserati also had experienced crippling financial losses from unpaid machine tool sales to Venezuela and a failed venture in Mexico. Maserati entered into voluntary reorganization, a form of bankruptcy overseen by the Italian government.

The Orsi family remained in control of Maserati, but the restrictions of the reorganization limited expenditures to only the most essential for the business to survive. Racing was out of the question. As a result of the restrictions, however, Maserati quickly showed signs of health before the end of 1958. Perhaps it would be possible to race once again.

Maserati Chief Engineer Guilo Alfieri's first assignment upon joining Maserati in 1953 had been to complete the design of the 250F. He was intimately involved with the ongoing development of the 250F to its World Championship level in 1957. He was responsible for the sports cars, as well, including the 300S and the 450S that came so close to winning the Sports Car World Championship. Even more significant, Alfieri had overseen the design of the Maserati 3500GT, the firm's first true production car and one that Maserati now relied on to save the company.

working hours. The limitations quickly became apparent. Reliance on existing components meant that yhe car would have to be front-engined, and – while Alfieri was knowledgeable about monocoque construction, and preferred it – the required specialized aircraft technology and developments costs to design a monocoque

The rear suspension came directly from the 250F, with a transverse leaf spring, De Dion tube and five-speed transaxle. The front suspension was fully independent and similar to the 250F. The 2-liter engine was laid to its side at a 45-degree angle to lower height, necessitating design of a new sump. The double-over-

Above: Moss perceived Piero Taruffi as a nemesis early in his career, but Taruffi (center, flanked by Moss and Gurney) later brought much needed stability to the CAMORADI team. Right: Stirling Moss was responsible for much of the testing with the Birdcage, which convinced him it was the car to beat in 1960. He is shown here on the way to his fourth victory in the Nürburgring 1000 km, codriving with Dan Gurney in 1960.

The restrictions of the reorganization specified that no money be spent directly on racing. Only support of customers racing their own cars was to be indulged. Alfieri was given approval by Omer Orsi to proceed with the design of a new race car within these limitations.

Historian Joel Finn described Alfieri's design brief for the new car: "Build a competitive car, at low cost, utilizing existing components wherever possible, for customer use. The factory would not race the car, only customers. With these constraints, the chances for success (were) slim, but Alfieri was both clever and resourceful."

In an interview with Finn in 1978, Alfieri described how he worked on the project at Maserati after regular

chassis were not available to him.

Alfieri laid down plans for a 2-liter competition car. This was a popular category for Italian racers, and he envisioned a ready market. As his starting point, he took the engine from the Maserati 200SI. The chassis design followed directly and logically on the design of the 250F, a tubular space frame made up of small-diameter sections triangulated for strength. As the 250F design evolved, this method had produced an increasingly lightweight racer. Alfieri took the method to the extreme for the new sports car, with a chassis made up of more than 200 individual tubes welded into a complete form that weighed only 66 pounds.

head camshaft head was also extensively modified to reverse the intake and exhaust sides. The completed car was bodied with aluminum shaped over thin steel rods, following typical Italian practice.

The car was designated Tipo 60. Loyal Guerrino Bertocchi first drove the car on his favorite test road from Modena to Verona on May 8, 1959. Less than two weeks later Stirling Moss was asked to test the prototype (s/n 2451) at Modena immediately after the Monaco Grand Prix. As Joel Finn described the test, "(Moss) was particularly impressed with the incredibly light yet precise steering, excellent neutral handling characteristics, superb brakes and the way it felt glued to the track." Moss suggested that the prototype be brought to the Nürburgring, where he could test it further during practice for the 1,000-km race on June 7, in which he would be driving for Aston Martin.

Moss broke the 2-liter lap record in the Nürburgring test during practice, before going on to win the 1,000-km race in the Aston Martin the following day. The Tipo 60 was entered by the Maserati factory, in a 2-liter sports-car race before the Formula Two grand prix at Rouen, France, on July 12, 1959, in order to prove the car's competitiveness and encourage orders from private teams. Moss was again the driver and won a convincing victory. Orsi made the decision to lay down six chassis. The Tipo 60's debut at Rouen was also important because pundits immediately began to consign nicknames to the car's unusual construction, which that eventually became known as the "Birdcage."

However, orders for the car didn't materialize as expected from 2-liter competitors in Italy. Stories credit the decision to upgrade the Tipo 60 to three liters differently, but facts seem to support that the first firm order came from Joe Lubin of Los Angeles, Calif. – for a 3-liter car. Lubin was only the first of many to see the potential for the new Maserati in the SCCA's most important D-Modified class for sports cars between 2,000-3,000cc. Coincidentally, the World Sports Car Championship was also contested by 3-liter cars.

Orsi approved the development of a larger engine. Alfieri responded by producing 2,890 cc from the smaller engine with a different bore and stroke, mak-

Above: Jim Clark in an Aston Martin DBR1 left the Porsches and Ferraris standing at the start of the 1960 Nürburgring 1000 km. The Porsche RS60s had previously won overall at Sebring and the Targa Florio. Below: The CAMORADI team entered two Tipo 61s for the 1960 Nürburgring 1000 km, one for Moss/Gurney and a second car for Masten Gregory and Gino Munaron.

ing revisions to the carburetors at the same time. The larger engine went into the six cars already under construction, which became known as Tipo 61s.

Moss described the Tipo 60/61 transformation to the author in 2008: "The original car was a very nice car to drive but it hadn't got enough power. The handling was excellent. But the Tipo 61 was a very, very good car. Plenty of torque. And it had a very rigid chassis. It was one of (Maserati's) best efforts."

CAMORADI

Enter Lloyd "Lucky" Casner. Casner was an American, born in New York and graduated from the University of Miami in Florida where, he became a transport pilot for Pan-American airlines. Although still something of an enigma today, Casner is credited with creating one of the first international racing teams overtly funded by sponsorship.

The name CAMORADI stood for CAsner MOtor RAcing DIvision. Despite its international-sounding name, CAMORADI was funded by American dollars. Casner first offered a $5 membership to enthusiasts, who received a membership card, a decal and a news-

Above: A young Dan Gurney contemplates during practice for the 1960 Nürburgring 1000 km. Early helmet and coveralls gave little protection compared with today. Below: The Maserati 8CTF was developed for 1938 Grand Prix racing with financial support from the Orsi family. Although the 8CTF was not competitive with the state-sponsored Mercedes-Benz and Auto Unions, Wilbur Shaw won the 1939 and 1940 Indianapolis 500 races in one of the three 8CTFs built for GPs (s/n 3032).

letter. When these contributions proved underwhelming, Casner approached Goodyear, then known as a stodgy manufacturer of passenger-car tires, to sponsor his team and demonstrate Goodyear's new line of high-performance sports-car tires.

With the support of Goodyear in his pocket, Casner went shopping for a suitable car to contest the 1960 World Sports Car Championship. He soon found himself in Modena testing Maserati's prototype Tipo 60 on the Autodrome. A deal was struck for CAMORADI to purchase two Tipo 61s for the 1960 race season. Alfieri and Bertocchi would provide technical support at major races.

Delivery of the two cars proved somewhat problematic, however, and CAMORADI first received the Tipo 60 prototype (2451) converted to Tipo 61 specs in November 1959. Author Finn: "True, he could have only one car but it was probably the fastest sports-racer in the

world and at half the price of any comparable machine. Lucky was certainly an appropriate nickname."

Eventually, CAMORADI took delivery of not one, but two additional Tipo 61s (s/n 2458 and s/n 2461) from a second production run of six cars, and another (s/n 2464) before Sebring.

1960 NÜRBURGRING 1,000 KM

The 1960 season was one of great change in international racing. Aston Martin announced its retirement from racing after winning the 1959 24 Hours of Le Mans and the World Sports Car Championship, making drivers Stirling Moss and Carroll Shelby available for sports-car races. Dan Gurney's departure from Ferrari to BRM for 1960 also freed him of sports-car commitments. American Masten Gregory lost his seat with Cooper and was similarly available. Casner snapped them all up. With only five races counting toward the championship and

both Ferrari and Porsche boycotting the Sebring race because of a dispute over fuel sponsorship, together with the speed the Birdcage had already shown, the team looked like world-beaters.

How quickly the 1960 season turned upside-down has been well documented. The CAMORADI Birdcages were fast, often qualifying first and setting the fastest lap of the race. But a series of recurring mechanical failures took them out of every race – usually in the lead – with the exception of the nonchampionship Grand Prix of Cuba won by Moss (2458). In particular, the team was plagued with a series of engine failures caused by a burst external oil line if the engine was not warmed up properly.

The team arrived at the Nürburgring in late May on the heels of this series of misfortunes. Any hope of the championship already was lost.

A total of 84 cars were entered for the 1960 1,000 km and the competition was stiff. Moss and Gurney were entered in the CAMORADI Birdcage 2461, plus a second car for Gregory and Gino Munaron. Ferrari entered Formula One drivers Phil Hill, Wolfgang von

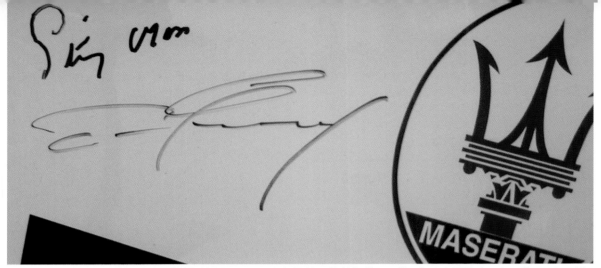

comment from Guerrino Bertocchi after the race was as satisfying as the difficult victory. "He was Fangio's mechanic. (And) he gave me a lot of credit for not hurting the engine. It was mostly because of my own experience building my own engines. But it meant a great deal to me."

Californian Carl Moore acquired 2461 in 2005 and vigorously races the car in West Coast vintage events, including the Monterey Historics. Updates continue to be made to the car without sacrificing its historic significance. "My interest is still in racing (the Birdcage)," he said. For those watching the CAMORADI Birdcage compete, the sight captures a moment in time – a once-in-a-lifetime moment when it all came together.

Below: The 1960 Nürburgring 1000 km-winning CAMORADI Birdcage was reunited with drivers Sir Stirling Moss and Dan Gurney in 2007, shown here with current caretaker Carl Moore of California. Opposite: Moore regularly competes in vintage races with 2461, including the Monterey Historics.

Trips, Cliff Allison and Willy Mairesse. Three Aston Martin DBR1s were privately entered, including the Border Reivers car for Jim Clark and 1959 Le Mans winner Roy Salvadori. Porsche RS60s, although in the under-2-liter category, had won overall victories in the previous two races, at Sebring and the Targa Florio.

A notable change to the CAMORADI team was the addition of Piero Taruffi as team manager. Nonetheless, practice started badly. Asked to recall the event nearly 50 years later, Moss referred to his famously detailed diaries. Day one: "Maser was awful. Raised the gear ratio and it was better. Seat is good. Screen lousy." The next day was no better. "Dan did two laps and an oil pipe broke. I didn't get to go out in the car. Goodyear tires on the front, Pirellis rear." The last comment demonstrates just how desperately the Goodyear-funded team was struggling.

Moss's diary continues succinctly on the morning of the race: "Arrived at 8:00 a.m. Circuit wet." Racing historian Janos Wimpffen describes the weather in more detail in his encyclopedic history of sports-car racing, *Time and Two Seats*: "The mist and fog of early morning stayed right where it was as the race began. At one stage the visibility was so poor that spectators had difficulty seeing across the track."

At the start, Moss got away first. At the quarter distance, Moss led two Porsches and two Ferraris in the top five. The CAMORADI team made a good first pit stop, and Gurney took over from Moss. On the track, Gurney maintained – even extended – the lead Moss had established, in only his third race at the 'Ring. Then the Birdcage cockpit suddenly was splashed with oil.

"I realized it was a scavenger line," Gurney recalled. "It occurred about seven miles from the pits. I looked at the oil pressure and it was ok. I thought to myself, 'I'm going to use the engine as lightly and as carefully as I can.' In some sections I actually shut the engine off."

Gurney continued to recall the scene when he finally reached the pits. "Bertocchi tried to bounce his hand off his forehead, as if to say the engine was kaput. But I managed to convince all of them that we still had a chance." The pit stop cost the team five-and-a-half minutes and the lead. Gurney returned to the track behind Hill in a Ferrari and Jo Bonnier in one of the Porsches. In what was to become one of the greatest drives of his career, "Gurney took back 30 seconds per lap from the two leaders in the densest fog and mist of the day," wrote Wimpffen. The car dropped to third once again during pit stops before Moss drove on to the victory.

The CAMORADI team had won its only championship victory of the once-promising 1960 season.

Nearly half a century later, Gurney described that a

1907 Wayne Model N Touring
"The Car That Takes You Through"

General "Mad Anthony" Wayne, though not known all that widely today, was one of America's Revolutionary War heroes. As a 34-year-old brigadier general, his most brilliant exploit was the storming of Stony Point on July 16, 1779, the strongest British post on the Hudson River. His forces, 150 strong, surprised 500 British solders with a night attack using only bayonets. In 1792, President Washington was concerned foreign powers might invade America. After disasterous confrontations with the Miami Indian nation under the leadership of Blue Jacket of the Shawnees and Little Turtle of the Miamis, who were consistently incited by the British, the U.S. was appeared to be weak and ripe for an attack from France, Spain or even England. Washington recalled Major General Wayne from civilian life and appointed him commander-in-chief of the United States Army, with the focus of taking control of the Northwest Territory (Ohio, Indiana and Michigan). After a year of reorganizing the army and another year of building a chain of forts, Wayne's troops defeated the Miami Confederacy in the Battle of Fallen Timbers (Toledo), ultimately ending British power on American soil forever. The victory had far-reaching implications, as another American defeat would surely have diminished the power of the U.S. government and possibly rendered the country incapable, at least perceptively, of protecting its citizens. The following year, Wayne signed the Treaty of Greenville with the Indians, giving most of what is now Ohio to the U.S. and clearing the way for that state to enter the Union in 1803.

BY WEST PETERSON

eports of Wayne's personality vary from impetuous to vain, but he inspired loyalty among his men. He was a shrewd politician but a weak businessman. His daring military exploits earned him the sobriquet "Mad Anthony." Unfortunatly, only one year after the signing of the Treaty of Greenville, Wayne was stricken with gout and died at the age of 51. A hero, Wayne's name now appears on counties in 13 states – on no less than 15 townships, villages, or cities, including Fort Wayne, Ind.; two forts; a college and a university; numerous streets, roads and secondary schools; a school bus manufacturer and a national forest. His nickname did not escape those with naming rights, as the Mad River, a tributary of the Great Miami

River in Dayton, Ohio, was also named after him.

Late-19th-century automobile pioneer William E. Kelly knew of General Wayne's reputation. When it came time for putting a suitable name on his upstart company, Kelly had no problems hooking onto the hero's moniker, even including renderings of Wayne in uniform on company literature and manuals along with his legendary words to Washington before storming Stony Point, "General, I'll storm hell, if you will plan it."

A machinist by trade, Kelly began experimenting with a vertical 4x4-inch, single-cylinder, gas-engine design as early as 1895. The following year he designed a two-cylinder marine engine with opposed

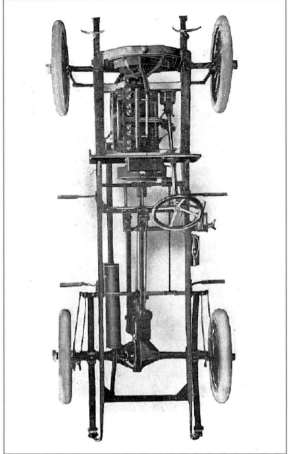

cranks, giving two working strokes in one shaft revolution and none in the next. Both of these engines, according to an article in the October 1904 issue of *Cycle and Automobile Trade Journal*, were still operating as stationary engines when the article was written. He put his first full car on the road in 1901, using yet a new engine design with a bore/stroke of 5x6 inches. Unfortunately, with this engine there was too much vibration, and he wasn't happy with the results.

Kelly organized the Wayne Automobile Company in 1902 and refined and built a second car, with a single horizontal cylinder, to show potential investors. Liking what they saw, E.A. Skae, Roger J. Sullivan, J.B. Brook

The 1907 Wayne Model N (shown here) represented a break in tradition in automotive design. With an all-metal body mounted to a pressed steel frame carrying complete power equipment, there was no subframe. In addition, tubular front and rear axles differed from the more traditional I-beam construction, and the employment of a rear transaxle must have been one of the first uses of such.

and Charles F. Palms bought in and got Wayne off the ground. Palms was the grandson of Francis Palms, an immigrant from Antwerp who amassed a great fortune as a banker, businessman, lumberman and real estate developer, and perhaps the largest landowner in Michigan during his lifetime. There's even a small town in Michigan's "thumb" named after him. His heirs followed in his footsteps and continued investments, development, banking and philanthropy.

With sound financial backing, Kelly's car was shown at the New York and Chicago exhibitions in January and February of 1904 with a price of $1,000. In his small "factory" on Dubois and Franklin streets, just east of downtown Detroit and a few blocks from the Detroit River, Kelly couldn't possibly build all the cars that were ordered. In addition, he wasn't completely sold on the single-cylinder engine with its obvious "impulses," so he dumped the idea even before the auto shows were closed.

Kelly's two-cylinder, 16-horsepower design had the general appearance of the standard opposed two-cylinder engine, but he gave the valves a vertical movement by introducing bell cranks in the valve linkage. This greatly increased the valve durability and eliminated

the need to regularly regrind. With consistently tight valves, there was no power loss. The first Wayne-employed chain drive was built on an 80-inch wheelbase and cost $1,200 (without top and head lamps). The five-passenger Model A touring was similar in size to the curved-dash Oldsmobile and was moderately successful.

Appearing in 1905, a Model C, rear-entrance, detachable tonneau utilizing the same two-cylinder engine but built on a 90-inch wheelbase was added to the lineup and cost $1,250 ($100 extra for top and headlamps). In addition, Wayne introduced its first four-cylinder engine with its 24hp Model B touring riding on a wheelbase of 102 inches and costing $2,000 (without accessories).

A new three-story brick plant was erected on a five-acre lot on the northwest corner of Piquette Avenue and Brush Street, just a block away from the then-new Ford plant also located on Piquette Avenue. With the capabilities of keeping up with demand, several two- and four-cylinder models were added to the lineup in 1906. Heading the list of two-cylinder cars was an economical 14hp Model H two-passenger runabout priced at just $800 and built on a new 82-inch wheelbase chas-

The Model N chassis featured a twin-ignition, 35hp, L-head, four-cylinder engine, and in an early use of a transaxle, its three-speed sliding gear transmission was mounted directly to the differential.

company boasted, "In placing the 1907 Wayne before the public we have striven to produce a car that would lead all competitors. The refinements marking the Wayne in the past have been retained. Every improvement that engineering and constructive skill could devise has been incorporated. Only the best materials that money can buy, executed by the most skillful mechanics obtainable, enter into it.

"No other car on the market has so many strong points that appeal to the discriminating, none so many that will commend themselves to the prospective purchaser seeking the best.

"As a finished product the Wayne commands admiration and compels the admission that no such values are to be found elsewhere for anything like the price. For luxuriousness, for simplicity of construction, reducing to a minimum the possibility of trouble, for

sis. A Model G four-passenger touring was built on the same chassis and priced at $1,000. The carryover Model C touring received an increase in horsepower, up to 20, but its price remained at $1,250

Three completely different four-cylinder cars were offered in 1906, including the Model B five-passenger touring built on a 102-inch wheelbase, powered by a 24/28hp engine and costing $2,000. The more powerful Model K five-passenger touring was built on a 100-inch wheelbase chassis, was powered by a 35hp engine and was priced at $2,500 (which included headlights). The big car, the Model F, was a five-passenger touring built on a 117-inch wheelbase, provided 50 horsepower and was priced at $3,500 (including headlights). A Model F limousine was also available for $4,500.

Changes abounded again in 1907. In management, crack body-builder Byron "Barney" Everitt became president of Wayne after selling Everitt Carriage Trimming Co. to Walter O. Briggs, who had been the manager. (Briggs went on to supply automobile bodies and products to several companies through the years.)

In production, all two-cylinder models were dropped, along with the Model F and B four-cylinder cars. In the "Foreword" of the factory literature, the

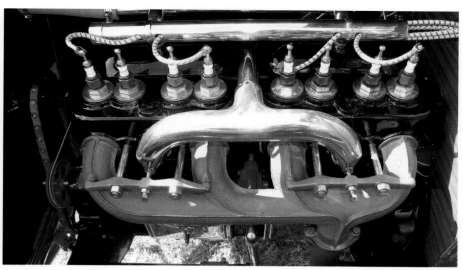

The 1907 Wayne Model N was powered by a 35hp, L-head four-cylinder engine. The 1908 Wayne Model "Thirty" was essentially the same car. This car, purchased from the Barney Pollard collection in 1974, is believed to be the only Model N in existence.

wearing qualities, for ability to meet every require-ment, the Wayne stands pre-eminent, challenging comparison with any automobile either of American or foreign make."

A luxurious Model R touring riding on a 117-inch wheelbase was the top-of-the-line Wayne that year, costing $3,500 (top extra). According to the literature, its side-entrance Pullman body had an additional pair of revolving chairs in front of the "tonneau seats," allow-ing room for seven passengers. In addition, a rather spacious compartment was easily reached through a door under the tonneau seat, making the Model R "an ideal machine for touring as well as general purpose." Other features included its 50-horsepower engine, with cylinders cast in pairs, that was allowed to be cradled to the rear of the drop-forged steel I-beam front axle via offset 40-inch semi-elliptic springs. Transferring power to the rear axle was a sliding gear, three-speed transmission with direct drive in high. Stopping the behemoth was through a single, external-band brake connected to a foot pedal, with two internal, expanding hub brakes connected to a hand-brake lever at the side of the operator.

A similar Model K was also offered. According to the factory, "from the standpoint of general construc-tion, workmanship and beauty ... the chief difference lies in the motor, wheelbase, wheels, tires and springs, which are a trifle smaller because of the decreased weight of the car." Like its R brethren, it was richly upholstered, but with passenger capacity limited to just five passengers. As in the previous-year Model K, it was powered by a 35-horsepower engine and utilized the sliding gear transmission. Brakes and suspension were the same as the Model R.

While the all-new, 35hp Model N built on a 106-inch wheelbase chassis (our feature car) was not as powerful as the Model R, it was distinctive and marked "a notable advance in the science of automobile con-struction." One of those features was the placement of the gearbox on the rear axle (a transaxle!), making the three-speed, sliding-gear transmission an integral part of the bevel gear housing, "thus insuring correct rela-tive positions of the gearing under all conditions." This gave the 36-inch-long driveshaft "an exceptionally low angle, being only 2.5 degrees maximum, and nothing with a load when the car is standing ... eliminating all friction between the engine and transmission, thereby conserving power."

Under the hood, the L-head engine had an aluminum crankcase and two pair of cylinder jugs with integral water jackets.. With dependability in mind, a high-ten-sion, vibrator, coil ignition (with storage batteries) and an external oiler were implemented.

The front axle, rather than being of I-beam con-struction, is a two-inch (outside dimension) steel tube, with drop-forged steel yokes, and steel casting, spring perches, pinned and brazed to the axle tube, which is dropped three inches in the middle. The rear axle is also built of steel tube flanges and three pieces of aluminum castings housing the gear casing and transmission.

A well-built, new-for-the-time, straight-line-type body was utilized, with steel and aluminum used throughout. Standard upholstery color was black leath-er with a carmine body, but customers could order any other finish at extra cost.

The 12 x 2-inch rear brake drums contained four brakes. The two exterior Raymond-type bands were operated by the hand lever, which first disengaged the clutch before applying braking pressure. The two internal toggle expanding bands worked through the right foot pedal.

Some 700 cars were built by Wayne in 1907, not a bad figure for a manufacturer of well-built, medium- to high-priced cars of the time. For 1908, Wayne offered just one Model, the "Thirty," in three body styles

There are numerous streets, schools, counties and cities named after "Mad Anthony" Wayne in no less than 13 states, but very few people know who the man was. William Kelly, founder of the Wayne Automobile Company in Detroit, knew full well who he was, and named his company after the Revolutionary War hero.

the role of chief engineer. Problems within the ranks caused a split in 1909, and by 1912, E-M-F was completely owned by Studebaker. However, that's a story for another day. The factory, a nicely designed structure, unfortunately went up in flames in June of 2005.

The 1907 Wayne Model N on these pages came out of the well-known Barney Pollard Collection in Detroit. Pollard was an early collector who gathered up hundreds of cars in the late 1920s and '30s. The scrap drives for the WWII war effort made it unpatriotic to

Wayne

"The car that takes you through"

Model N. 30-35 H. P., $2,500

Selective type sliding gear transmission, located on rear axle.
Three speeds forward and reverse, direct drive on high speed.
All working parts easily accessible.
Simplicity and strength making it trouble proof.
Metal body. Exceptionally roomy tonneau.
Only the best materials procurable.

Other Waynes are Model R, 50 H. P., seven passenger touring car with Pullman body, selling at $3,500, and Model K, 35 H. P., five passenger car, selling at $2,500—both great values.

CATALOGUE SENT UPON REQUEST.

WAYNE AUTOMOBILE COMPANY
Dept. 10, Detroit, Michigan

– a five passenger touring, a four-passenger tourabout, and a two-passenger roadster, all priced at $2,500 and equipped with the 35hp, four-cylinder powerplant. It was, essentially, the same as the Model N of 1907.

Early in the year, Walter Flanders, production manager at Ford, walked down Piquette Avenue and became the new manager of Wayne. In June, Wayne merged with Northern Automobile Co. and became E-M-F., the initials standing for the new company's principals: Barney Everitt; William Metzger, a marketing guru from Cadillac and a cofounder of the first Detroit auto show in 1899; and Walter Flanders. The goal was to build a mass-produced, medium-priced vehicle utilizing the strengths of each, with William Kelly playing

keep junk cars, but Pollard was one of the few who recognized them as more than scrap iron. He hid them in numerous places and stacked them like dominoes on their frame ends, nose down, hanging from the rafters. Pollard died in the early 1970s, and many cars were sold at auction in 1974. His children still

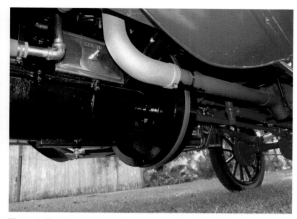

"this car even had the wires on the timer ... the door latches ... the spring oiler drive; it had everything! We replaced some wood on the lower body and made some new panels. After using some hi-tech paint removers that took off the varnish finish, we rubbed the original paint until we had good samples of the original colors and all the pinstriping. We even had enough upholstery to use as good patterns.

One of the biggest challenges was the engine, where Dunning found a broken crankshaft and crankcase. While it was easy to find someone who could make a crankshaft, it proved to be expensive. Fitted with new and improved bearings and a rewelded crankcase, Dunning had a good-running engine. He was rewarded for the splendid restoration, done in his own shop, with an AACA national award, the AACA Cup, during the club's February 2006 Annual Meeting in Philadelphia. △Q

Wayne challenged comparison with any automobile, either of American or foreign make. Note the creative use of the rear door hinges, allowing the door to swing away from the fender. The Model N came standard with a horn, mats, tools and five lamps, including two sidelamps, two headlamps and a taillamp. The top was roughly $100 extra.

own several of the ultra-rare cars, and sales from the collection are far and few between.

The Wayne was purchased at the 1974 auction by a Canadian who had intentions of restoring it. After several years of postponing its resurrection, in 1999, the car was offered to Jack Dunning, Cambridge, Ohio. What appealed to Dunning was the fact that the car was complete and totally unmolested, although in deplorable condition. It had all the ingredients of a great restoration project. Even though many parts had to be fabricated, having all the originals for patterns made it relatively easy. According to Dunning,

Patterson
Perfection

Stories, James A. Patterson explained, have no place in his collection. He collects cars that are unusually beautiful and are original works, not combinations of several cars.

BY NED LAWLER
PHOTOGRAPHY BY NED J.
& KATE LAWLER

The most notable example of the lengths required to assemble an original car fit for Jim Patterson's collection is his 1939 Bugatti 57C, with the distinctively flowing roadster body by Karosserie Voll & Ruhrbeck of Berlin-Charlottenburg, Germany. To understand the significance of this car in its present restored condition, let's time travel through the 12 major steps to get the car to the collection. The Patterson Collection, in concert with RM Classic Cars, has documented the following history.

3. Upon completion, the avant-garde car was sold to an unknown person; the car carried Berlin registration numbers. The single grille badge on the body, which remains on the car today, hints of its past. In the last two years before World War II, the car was at the disposal of three-time Olympic gold medal skater Sonja Henie. The "Berlin Ice Skating Club" is the translation of the wording on the badge, and it certainly could have been attached during her association with the car.

4. The car was hidden away during the war and turned up in 1946 in an unclaimed auto impound in Munich.

5. Then entered Tadeusz Tabincki, Polish Minister of Transportation and member of the secret police. During his reign, his credentials allowed him to wander through postwar Germany searching for cars that had been "stolen" from Poland and have them repatriated. Such was the case for #57819 and about 100 other significant cars. He cloistered these finds in his private collection until the late 1960s, when he quietly started selling them into Western Europe.

Left: 1939 Bugatti Type 57C Voll & Ruhrbeck Cabriolet participating in the Pebble Beach Tour d'Elegance 2006. Above: Jim Patterson Sr. inspects the 1937 Talbot Lago 150C. Below: The "Black and Tans" from front to rear: '39 Type 57C Bugatti, '37 Talbot Lago 150C, '36 Delahaye 135, '37 Peugeot Darl'mat 402, '39 Delage D8-120S.

1. The chassis #57819 arrived in Düsseldorf, Germany, fresh from the factory, to the attention of the German Bugatti importer, Mr. Knoll, on April 26, 1939. Being one of the final Type 57 chassis produced and the last one delivered in Germany, it had the dual-lobe Rootes-style "compressor" and competent hydraulic brakes.

2. After a short two-day admiration of the chassis, it was transported to the Voll & Ruhrbeck works, where it was entrusted to the care of Carl Otto Offelsmeyer, whose ability to blend his knowledge of aerodynamics and art produced a body contour that has visual appeal from any angle viewed. It's thought that this is the only Bugatti to carry German coachwork.

6. Belgian Bugatti dealer Jean de Dobbeleer traveled to the Tabincki collection to purchase #57819 and returned across the Soviet-guarded border with the engine and assorted parts. One can only speculate that he felt the need to return with as much of the car as possible to protect his investment or that parts of cars were easier to take across the border. In any case, a few months later the balance of the car arrived in his shop for recommissioning.

7. September of 1969 found the car being sold in Germany to Uwe Hucke, who had the Voll & Ruhrbeck body removed and the chassis fitted with an Atlantic-style reproduction body.

8. The original body was left in the care of Helmet Feierabend, where it was stored in the corner of his Wurtzburg, Germany, shop. We will put aside the original body and follow the rebodied chassis.

9. In 1975, the car was in the hands of Johnny Thuysbaert, whose large frame didn't fit the cramped cabin, so he passed along the car.

Above: 1937 Peugeot Darl'mat 402 Coupe. This series of cars was a collaboration among auto dealer and visionary Emile Darl'mat, gifted designer Georges Paulin and body maker Marcel Pourtout. Below: Two pieces of art, the 1947 Talbot Lago T26 Cabriolet created by Figoni et Falaschi and captured on canvas by renowned English automotive artist Barry Rowe.

10. The hapless customized #57819 languished in a Swiss restoration shop, where the engine, serial number 90C, was rebuilt, but time was never found to complete a restoration.

11. As the 21st century opened, Jim Patterson set out to reassemble one of the most unique and striking Type 57 Bugattis. He was able to secure the chassis, but as he described this purchase, it was "buying the crackers before you could be sure of getting the peanut butter." After having the crackers in the can, he set off for the peanut butter.

12. The stalwart German wasn't sure he wanted to part with the body, but after months of discussion and negotiation, the desire to see the car reunited won him over. There was a caveat, however. He wanted payment in strong – at that time – U.S. dollars. After explaining that carrying a briefcase laden with cash across borders in the era of terrorist activity was not practical, Herr. Feierabend relented to a more conventional transfer of funds, and the Patterson Collection had the pieces to assemble the sandwich.

The ensuing restoration by RM Classic Cars was completed to the high standards of Patterson in both authenticity and craftsmanship. Because the body had set in dry storage for nearly four decades, much was usable, but it was disassembled down to the very basic components, and each piece of frame timber and body metal was analyzed and reassembled using every bit of original material that was practical. After the mechanical and cosmetic restoration of the rolling chassis, the body was lowered on the frame and

entered in the premier American concours at Pebble Beach, where it was awarded Best in Class and the Gwenn Graham Award for Most Elegant Convertible. In the final four for Best of Show, it finished just a wisp of exhaust away from the top slot. The 2007 Amelia Island Concours presented the Bugatti with The Compass Bank Award for The Best Open Car as the bright Florida sun dazzled the paint and bright work. At the Motor City's Meadow Brook Concours later in the summer of 2007, the Best in Class and Chairman's Award were passed to Patterson. The Queen City of Cincinnati hosts the Ault Park Concours, and in 2008 the sleek black beauty went home with the Best of Show. Certainly the international classic car community has rewarded the noble quest to bring back this rolling art treasure.

store. He was self-sufficient from that point onward. As a young lad making his deliveries, he remembers being impressed by the beautiful cars executives were driving downtown, but his early life had no time or money for such baubles.

Young Patterson learned multitasking very early, but at that time it was called survival. Additionally, the ability to maximize his current situation to create the path to the next level was developed. His high school athletic ability gained him a baseball scholarship to the University of Louisville. Air Force ROTC provided a commission in the Air Force after completing his marketing degree. The Air Force developed his management skills, and his frugal nature allowed him to save for investing in his future. In 1959, after completing his Air Force commitment as a captain, he entered

The Maharaja's Mercedes, 1937 540K Sindelfingen Cabriolet A shown with the 5.4 liter straight 8 with "on demand" supercharging.

slipped into position as if it had never left, much to the delight of all involved.

When the final product, finished in black and tan, was taken to the show grounds, the experts agreed that this was indeed a marvelous restoration and noteworthy reuniting of 57819. Shown at the elite Concorso d'Eleganza Villa d'Este on Italy's Lake Como in April 2006, it was awarded the Coppa d'Oro Villa d'Este, or "Gold Cup," that is voted by the entrants themselves. Following the Italian adventure, the Type 57C was

As the history of the Bugatti was unfolding across the Atlantic, Jim Patterson's own timeline was developing. A child of the Great Depression, he grew up in a modest family home in Louisville, Ky. Their house, as he describes, was comprised of four rooms but because the stove would only heat three, the last room remained closed. Jim could be the poster boy for "the harder I worked, the luckier I became." At the age of 12, he started his working life as a drugstore delivery boy and janitor for a dry goods

the restaurant business as a franchisor of Jerry's restaurants. The restaurant business was self-taught by a crash course of working every day but Christmas for several years. Had his signature not been on the loan, he might have left the business during several particularly tough times. In the end, hard work prevailed and eight years later he had three units in operation.

After obtaining his master's degree from Jerry's school of hard knocks, he discovered English-style fish and chips. It was such a revelation compared to the ter-

One of Patterson's holdings, Western Restaurants, operates more than 50 Wendy's franchises.

If this sounds like a Horatio Alger rags-to-riches saga, the Horatio Alger Association thinks so too, and in 2002, it awarded a membership to Patterson. These memberships are awarded to people who have risen over a humble beginning to be leaders in their field. On the other side of the balance sheet are multiple entries where the Pattersons have given back, providing individual scholarships and supporting educational institu-

Top: Talbot Lago 150C engine, a 4.0-liter pushrod straight 6 with triple carburation. Right: The two English gentlemen, a 1959 Rolls Royce James Young aluminum-bodied drop head convertible sets to the left of the 1953 Bentley R-type Continental also in aluminum. Left: One of the custom features of this 1960 Ferrari 400 Super America, a "speedometer delete" dashboard to prevent the original owner's wife from knowing the speed. Bottom: Two timeless profiles, the 1959 Ferrari 250GT California poses in front of the '37 Bugatti Type 57C.

rible fish he remembered from his youth he wanted to bring it to market. Long John Silver's was born. Selling his Long John Silver's interest in 1975 provided capital for developing several other businesses in foodservice, computer software, telecommunications, oil and gas exploration, real estate development and insurance.

Above: The Glass Menagerie: Front to back Corvettes all, 1953 s/n #21, a '57 and '58, both fuel injected, two '67 427 " big block" cars, convertible and coupe, and a '67 special order COPO convertible. Below: Jim Paterson Jr. enjoys the view of the big iron in his '67 427 cubic-inch convertible.

#21, the Pattersons asked Tom to continue with them to manage the day-to-day maintenance and logistics of collecting classics. When shown, the car captured the Bloomington Gold Award in 1999 and several additional awards in succeeding shows. As the collection has grown, now exceeding 25 exceptional cars, Allen has been assisted by another craftsman, Brennan Doyle. This duo keeps the cars in Best of Show condition and ably ensures they make the shows.

Jim II's interest in collecting exposed his father to the excitement and rekindled his fascination with the beautifully shaped cars he remembered as a boy. Jim I is a curves-not-cams guy, stating that he's attracted to the visual grace of a car and apologizes for his lack of

tions at all levels. To list all the philanthropic work would take more space than the accomplishments. This affable, soft-spoken gentleman is indeed "lucky."

Patterson's son Jim II is the actual catalyst for the creation of the Patterson Collection. He, like his father, earned a marketing degree from the University of Louisville and cut his teeth in the restaurant business. After his foodservice experience, he gained knowledge in the advertising arena as a partner in an advertising agency. He then was involved in successful restructuring and creation of several business ventures and now is involved full-force with the various Patterson businesses. This provides both the close working environment necessary to foster business success and good communication concerning their automotive endeavors.

Jim II is a Corvette and muscle-car fan, and while he had a '67 Corvette 427 roadster, the purchase of a 1953 Corvette s/n 21 was the genesis of the operational collection. This car was one of the first batch of 25 Corvettes that were hand-built, and it required special restoration to insure that its provenance was not lost during the project. Craftsman Tom Allen was employed to do the restoration, and after the 18-month rebirth of

mechanical knowledge. With the collection of "French curves" he has assembled, his eye is very good and he need not be apologetic.

As the two discussed collecting, surrounded by their cars, Jim I noted that he has some visions of cars he wants to pursue, but he hasn't decided on exactly the object of his desire. However, he will continue in the vein of elegant bodies. Jim II is a bit more pragmatic, wanting great cars reliable enough to be taken out for an evening drive without being overly concerned about an octagenarian part failing. While he muses that any significant performance car is under consideration, the Corvette Grand Sport, Miura and Cobra are on the short list when he's ready to move the collection forward.

Advice on collecting? Jim II says to keep it simple, for the hobby can easily become a business with all the responsibilities of managing and none of the income. They agree that quality is key, and it's better to have one significant car of a given value than several lesser cars totaling the same investment.

The collection is housed in a contemporary building that has a gallery for the cars, a maintenance shop and a trailer bay that allows the trailer to be loaded inside. The mezzanine houses a library, a conference room and a balcony with a great view.

Almost every car has earned significant awards. The collection can be divided into groups with common elements, as follows.

The Patterson Collection

The "Black and Tans" is the group with the "swoop" and are finished in deep black with tan interiors. They are, for the most part, French.

- **1939 Bugatti 57C Voll & Ruhrbeck Roadster**
- **1937 Talbot Lago 150C** (Built originally as a proto type racer, it was rebodied by Figoni et Falaschi with the current touring body.)
- **1936 Delahaye 135 Competition Court Figoni et Falaschi Coupe** (This car shares its unusual fender line with only one other car, a roadster.)
- **1937 Peugeot Darl'mat 402 Coupe Body by Pourtout** (One of six coupes.)
- **1939 Delage D8-120S Letourneur et Marchand Aerosport Coupe**
- **1953 Bentley R-Type Continental Sports Saloon** (When new, this aluminum-bodied, high-speed tourer was the fastest production car.)
- **1926 Bugatti Type 56 Electric** (One of two remaining, this was a small battery-powered runabout that Bugatti built for himself, and only a small batch was constructed. This one belonged to Queen Elisabeth of Belgium.)

The Blue Benzes

- **1958 300SL Roadster**. (Finished in dark blue with blue-grey interior.)
- **1956 300SL Gullwing** (Restored to match the roadster, a stunning pair.)
- **1956 300SC Cabriolet**
- **1937 540K Cabriolet A** (One of a few right-hand-drive, this one commissioned by HRH The Maharaja of Indor.)

Fabulous in Fiberglass

- **1953 Corvette** (Serial No. 21 of the first 25 handmade cars.)
- **1957 Corvette** (This is a fuel-injected car.)
- **1958 Corvette** (Also a "fuelie.")
- **1967 Corvette Big block 427 convertible** (With removable hardtop.)
- **1967 Corvette 427 Coupe**
- **1967 Corvette convertible C.O.P.O** (A special-order 1967 car in the discontinued 1966 Mossport green color.)

The Italian Jobs

- **1959 Ferrari 250GT Tour de France Competition Berlinetta** (This was the last covered-headlight car. It has a strong competition history in the United States.)
- **1959 Ferrari 250GT California** (The long-wheelbase version with design by Pininfarina and body by Scaglietti.)
- **1960 Ferrari 400 Super America** (One of seven short-wheelbase versions, this one is "speedometer delete" so the wife wouldn't know how fast he was driving.)
- **1969 Ferrari 365 GTS** (One of the 17 located of 20 built.)
- **1967 Lamborghini 400GT** (One of the last of 23 "interim" versions of this model.)

Additional Excitement

- **1939 Delage D6 LM Grand Prix** (The one remaining of two Grand Prix cars built for the French races. It was raced pre- and postwar.)
- **1947 Talbot Lago T26 Cabriolet** (This distinctive two-tone blue Figoni et Falaschi body was a Hollywood favorite, and its caricature found its way into cartoon cars of the era.)
- **1959 Rolls Royce Silver Cloud** (James Young Drop Head Convertible. One of two aluminum convertibles built.)

The chassis of this 1937 Talbot Lago 150C ran in several major races in the 1936 season. It was rebodied in '37 as this flowing "one off" coupe, a sister car to a like roadster. As a tribute to Mr. Patterson's eye for style this car has won many awards, the most significant being the "People's Choice Award" at both the 2003 Louis Vuitton Classic in Paris and the 2006 Pebble Beach Concours d'Elegance.

Stuttgart Calling

I f the attraction of opposites is a valid phenomenon, it certainly applied to Ferdinand Porsche and Camillo Castiglioni. The two had known each other since the Trieste-born entrepreneur Castiglioni first burst on the Austro-Hungarian scene as a maker of rubberized fabrics for airships. The contrast between them couldn't have been greater: the youthful Castiglioni intent on multiplying his assets and the engineer, approaching middle age, intensely committed to transport technology on land, at sea and in the air.

After an epic Mercedes success in the 1924 Targa, from left, Christian Werner, Ferdinand Porsche and riding mechanic Karl Sailer.

BY KARL LUDVIGSEN

Nevertheless, they were friends. Porsche and Castiglioni addressed each other with the informal *du* that conferred intimacy. Theirs was a mutual admiration society, each acknowledging that the other had exceptional talents in his field that didn't threaten the other. This allowed them to pursue their aims jointly after the war, when Castiglioni's General Deposit Bank controlled Austro-Daimler. Reciprocally, the Wiener Neustadt company was one of the jewels of Castiglioni's holdings. And the banker knew that Ferdinand Porsche had made it so.

Of course Porsche was well aware that "CC" didn't always play by the rules. The two chanced to be on the same train from Vienna to Berlin when Castiglioni mysteriously suggested to Porsche that he join him in his private car, but only after they'd crossed the border. Having done so, the engineer then saw the entrepre-

neur reach into a hiding place to extract a valuable Old Master painting he'd smuggled duty-free into Germany. That Castiglioni was unafraid of exposing his machinations to Porsche spoke volumes about the trust the two men shared.

From 1919 onward, Ferdinand Porsche moved heaven and earth to provide employment for the more than 6,000 souls whose families were completely dependent on continuation of Wiener Neustadt's activities – without the benefit of orders from an empire fighting a major war. His was the total responsibility, as General Director, for all aspects of the company's activities. He kept not only Austro-Daimler but also the former aircraft factory, ÖFFAG, busy with contracts both at home and abroad. And when he had extra capacity he used it to develop new initiatives for the future.

Meanwhile, Camillo Castiglioni was just as active

in fields that interested him. Lingering Skoda participation in Austro-Daimler finally faded at the end of 1920, when Castiglioni began share exchanges to form "common interests" with two other Austrian enterprises, Fiat's licensee in Vienna and Graz's Puch, a maker of cars and motorcycles. Under Porsche's direction, this led to a money-saving sharing of activities in purchasing, sales and design.

With his majority holdings in BMW, Castiglioni was active abroad as well. When in 1920 Stuttgart's Daimler Motoren Gesellschaft raised money in the capital markets to finance its postwar reconstruction, the Italian acquired enough shares to make him a substantial minority investor. His attempts to wield even greater influence in DMG were foiled by the preference shareholding of the Deutsche Bank and its influential Chairman, Emil Georg von Stauss.

Less helpful to the home factory in Wiener Neustadt was Camillo Castiglioni's establishment of Austro-Daimler sales offices in major nations abroad. Here he'd taken a leaf from the Emil Jellinek book. Through these sales operations, separately controlled by his General Deposit Bank, he profited from the difference between the sales prices of the company's products and the transfer prices paid to Austro-Daimler. In fact, he used this means progressively to starve Wiener Neustadt of the funds it needed to expand and modernize.

Nevertheless, the decade started well. Reporting a profit for 1920, Austro-Daimler said that this was possible because "in spite of the still-prevailing general difficulties, which have an unfavorable effect on our production possibilities, our factory was able to gain new sales opportunities and, thereby, a broadening of the scope of our business." This was solely and completely the achievement of Ferdinand Porsche, who married product ranges old and new to give Austro-Daimler every opportunity to exploit new markets.

In addition to his work on road and racing versions of the small Sascha and his 2-liter Grand Prix racer, in 1922 Ferdinand Porsche was on the brink of launching his update of the AD 617, the ADV, and was well along in the engineering of his ADM, which would be a landmark design in automotive history. To boot, he

A cluttered exhibition in Vienna in 1923 showed cars that Porsche had worked hard to add to Austro-Daimler's offerings: two ADMs, in the background, and an ADV chassis. Wiener Neustadt would long benefit from these advanced Porsche designs.

The 1923 Mercedes Indianapolis entries were two-seaters just when the rules allowed single-seaters for the first time. Their unusual ducted exhausts, not perpetuated by Porsche, were ear-splitting. Otto Salzer used this one to win a hillclimb at Solitude, near Stuttgart, later in 1923.

was exploring the idea of giving the ADM an all-electric automatic transmission. Porsche combined both generator and electric motor in a single unit behind the engine, thus merging his Mixte ideas. From there the drive went to the rear wheels through an ordinary drive shaft and axle. He installed this advanced transmission in one of his ADM prototypes.

Meritorious though they were, Ferdinand Porsche's initiatives were also costly. They faced a strong headwind in spiraling inflation in both Austria and Germany. So desperate was the situation that Porsche discovered that the entire value of his life insurance would barely suffice to buy a pair of shoes.

Here was another situation that Castiglioni could and did exploit. Where hard currencies could be won in export markets, especially in England, he and his sales subsidiaries intercepted these and converted them into severely devalued Austrian crowns that were then remitted to Austro-Daimler. This was profoundly annoying to Porsche, who could only acquire specialized machine tools to upgrade the company's

manufacturing equipment if he had access to hard currencies. Struggle though he did to get his hands on foreign currency, Porsche was frustrated by Castiglioni's exchange-rate exploitation.

Tensions between the two men grew toward the end of 1922. Fritz Kuhn's tragic death at Monza became a stick with which to beat the engineer. Although Porsche could and did show that the car's crash was not the fault of his design, his board still blamed him for the wire wheel's failure and the loss of Kuhn. The driver's death and the cost of competing abroad, which would have eaten into Castiglioni's hoarded hard currency, were reasons enough for the Austro-Daimler board to decide to refrain from international racing in 1923.

Other issues arose when the research and development budget for 1923 was being prepared. Ferdinand Porsche's first submissions were rejected on the grounds of excessive cost at a time of poor business conditions, although a subtext would have been an attempt by the board to rein in what it saw as Porsche's excessive zeal for product improvement.

Circulated against him since springtime was the tale of an Austro-Daimler owner who brought his car in for repairs in late autumn. "Oh, that's an old model," he was told. "We've brought out four new models in the meantime and we no longer have spares for your car." Exaggerated for effect though this anecdote was, it did suggest a subordination of production efficiency to product improvement on a scale that an impoverished Austro-Daimler could not afford.

Picking up signs that his mentor was in trouble at Wiener Neustadt, Alfred Neubauer asked a friend what he thought. The friend waved off his concerns, saying, "The end of the world will come before Austro-Daimler parts with Porsche!" However, since springtime when Neubauer spoke with Camillo Castiglioni's son Arturo, he gained a different perspective. "Since the Monza catastrophe," he said, "Herr Porsche's position is tottering badly." His father was looking for an opportunity, Arturo added, "to draw a line under the Porsche chapter."

That opportunity came at a board meeting in Vienna in February of 1923. Castiglioni refused, again, to remit hard currencies directly to Austro-Daimler. Ferdinand Porsche's engineering budgets still lacked approval. Finally, Castiglioni laid down conditions that he must have been confident Porsche couldn't accept. Within two weeks, he said, it was the general director's task to slash the workforce by 2,000, fully one third of the staff. The engineer was furious, outraged. This would cut the heart from his already struggling company. Hurling imprecations at the board members – some say even hurling a candlestick – a choleric Porsche shouted, "I won't go along with that! And if you don't like it, you can carry on making your garbage on your own – without me!" and stormed from the boardroom, slamming the door.

It took the engineer three quarters of an hour to drive back to Wiener Neustadt. Arriving at the gates, he found his path blocked by a commercial official. He was told he wasn't allowed to enter the grounds. Not one to give up easily, Porsche arrived at work the next morning as usual. Soon a two-man delegation from the board confronted him. "Herr Porsche," one said, "we've decided to accept your resignation of yesterday." Exploiting the engineer's triphammer temper, Castiglioni had achieved his objective. Word swept through the factory, where the reaction was astonishment, incredulity. To an entire generation of Austrians, Ferdinand Porsche *was* Austro-Daimler.

On behalf of his chief, Alfred Neubauer felt moved to action. He traveled to Vienna, where he was received with warmth by Alexander "Sascha" Kolowrat. If any-

one could save the day, thought Neubauer, it would be the influential and enthusiastic Count. He implored Kolowrat to find a way to keep Porsche in his post, saying that "without him, Austro-Daimler is like a body without a soul!"

"You overestimate my potentialities," a thoughtful Kolowrat explained to Neubauer, adding that the divide between Porsche and Castiglioni had grown too large to be bridged. "But I'll do everything in my power," he said, "to secure for Porsche an honorable departure, which he has earned." Kolowrat's intervention gained better financial terms for the engineer. Porsche was also allowed to take three cars with him, including the advanced ADM Mixte, its electric transmission integrated with its driveline, mentioned earlier.

Engineering of Austro-Daimler cars was taken

To qualify for entry in the first-ever German Grand Prix on July 11, 1926, two of Porsche's eights were transformed into "sports cars" by the addition of vestigial rear seats, easy to do with the under-floor fuel tanks.

out to be the answer to everyone's dreams. Daimler had been a board member at DMG through 1920, but then was dropped from its ranks. When in 1922 the company rejected his plans for an eight-cylinder engine, Paul Daimler looked elsewhere. In July of that year he accepted the post of chief engineer at Horch.

DMG had been casting sidelong glances at Ferdinand Porsche for some time. At 1921's Brussels Salon, Daimler's Richard Lang was admiring the display chassis of Austro-Daimler's impressive new AD 617 when the Austrian company's production chief Otto Stahl, a fellow Swabian, ambled over. After some pleasantries, Lang, an engineer in his own right, asked Stahl, "Do you think Porsche could be moved to change to Untertürkheim?" Stahl reported the remark to Porsche, who at the time still hoped to realize his dreams in Austria.

The engineer knew that conditions in Germany weren't much better than they were in Austria. Alfred Neubauer described Germany's economic plight: "Stocks fell while prices and taxes rose, and almost daily another zero was added to the figures on our banknotes. You paid a million for a tram ride and a billion for a loaf of bread. Inflation roared through the exhausted nation. Sheer existence was obliterated, the wealthy melted like snow in sunshine and shrewd speculators profited from widespread destitution."

German inflation soared relentlessly from 1918. From

over by a Porsche acolyte, Karl Rabe, at the tender age of 27. Early in 1922, Rabe had been granted his degree in engineering. This earned him a warm letter of congratulation from Ferdinand Porsche, who was "extraordinarily pleased" by the news and sent his "heartiest congratulations." It would be Rabe's good fortune to launch both the ADV and the ADM and later, with his ADR, to exploit the ADM's potential with a backbone frame and swing-axle rear suspension. He found little need to change Porsche's superb six-cylinder engines.

Meanwhile, another chief engineer was falling foul of his board. Paul Daimler, whom Porsche had succeeded at Wiener Neustadt, wasn't getting on with his colleagues at Daimler Motoren Gesellschaft. He'd committed some of his company's models to Knight-patent, sleeve-valve engines, which were not turning

An older (top left) and a much younger Ferdinand Porsche. Above: Staff members of Anton Porsche's metalworking workshop posed for posterity in 1889. Ferdinand, then turning 14, is on the floor at the right.

its value of 4.2 to the dollar before the war, the mark fell to 49 at the end of 1919, 73 at the end of 1920 and 190 to the dollar at the close of 1921. Following a severe depression, the first chaotic collapse of Germany's currency occurred in 1922, which ended with a dollar worth 7,353 marks. Some stabilization occurred early in 1923, a year that closed, however, with the demoralizing absurdities related by Neubauer.

Lack of confidence in the currency was linked with failing confidence in Germany's postwar government. It was dubbed "Weimar" after the city in which its admirably democratic new constitution had to be drafted because conditions in Berlin were too disorderly at the time. During 1920, in fact, the government fled to Stuttgart and then returned to Berlin. Seen as the illegitimate offspring of a humiliating defeat in the war, the Weimar government struggled from crisis to crisis, battered on right and left by ultraconservative nationalists and ultraradical protocommunists. Relative stability only came at the end of 1923 when the respected Hjalmar Schacht was named to head the Reichsbank. In 1924, Schacht restored the mark to its former value of 4.2 to the dollar.

These were the turbulent economic conditions in which the Daimler Motoren Gesellschaft had to find its way after the war. It was led by an authentic veteran, Ernst Berge, as general director. Born in 1868, Berge was a businessman in Homburg before joining Daimler in 1902 as joint commercial director with Eduard Fischer at its restructured Österreichische Daimler Motoren Gesellschaft at Wiener Neustadt, where Paul Daimler was settling in as chief engineer. With Daimler, Berge came to Untertürkheim in 1905 and became a management-board member in 1907.

Ernst Berge was named DMG's general director during the company's dramatic wartime expansion. "From Berge's surviving business correspondence," wrote historian Bernard Bellon, "the picture emerges of a deliberate businessman who on occasion could be ruthless, be it with the state or with his workers." "The development of DMG into a world-class firm is closely associated with his name," the company later said of Ernst Berge. In the automotive field his post-

Porsche (on right) with his nephew on holiday before his death.

war policy resembled that of Austro-Daimler: to focus on the upper levels of the auto world instead of the potentially risky small-car market.

DMG and Berge were under the watchful eye of the supervisory board, chaired since 1910 by an enterprising banker, Alfred von Kaulla. Born in 1852, von Kaulla had proven his entrepreneurial skills at Stuttgart's Württemberg Vereinsbank, which had close and successful links with the Deutsche Bank. Called "an enterprising, bright, robust man," Alfred von Kaulla had been a DMG board member since 1902. As supervisory-board chairman, he took a close interest in all the automaker's affairs.

Here, Ferdinand Porsche was only too well aware, was another company in the hands of the bankers. The Deutsche Bank dominated its ownership, but his old friend Camillo Castiglioni was involved with a lesser shareholding. Also active was an ambitious Berlin car dealer and auto-body producer, Jakob Schapiro.

Although his main focus was on Benz in Mannheim, where he'd exploited the inflationary years to gain a 40-percent shareholding by 1923, Schapiro had also acquired a smaller package of Daimler shares.

In 1922 an investment in DMG wasn't looking all that brilliant. Strikes and the depression were slowing its postwar conversion. Production of cars and trucks of 1,171 in 1919 had grown to 2,152 in 1920, almost reaching the prewar record of 2,183 in 1912. Then output reversed to 1,875 in 1921 and only 1,342 in 1922, including fewer than 1,000 passenger cars. Although Paul Daimler's use of sleeve valves for some models and his pioneering of supercharging for production cars had been high-profile initiatives, these costly innovations hadn't caught on. Nor had Daimler bowed to his board's request that he launch at least one model with reasonable volume potential.

In mid-1922, DMG found itself without a chief engineer. Richard Lang was doing his best to stream-

In 1925, Porsche approved Wilhelm Werner's plan to rebuild one of the GP eights as a sprint machine. With an I-beam axle, larger radiator and rear-mounted fuel tank, it scored hillclimb successes in 1926, here in the hands of works driver Otto Merz.

line manufacturing at Untertürkheim, but its cupboard of future products was all but bare. With von Kaulla retiring from the supervisory board, Ernst Berge asked a neutral third party, Paul Eberspächer of the eponymous components firm, to sift the candidates and make a recommendation. Eberspächer, familiar with the impasse facing the company, argued that only a man of the topmost category could provide the products it needed. Ferdinand Porsche would be costly, he told the supervisory board, but he'd be worth it.

Checking Porsche's references, a newcomer to the supervisory board, Emil Georg von Stauss, contacted Castiglioni. The Italian would, after all, be well placed to assess the engineer. "You can take Porsche on," said the Austro-Daimler proprietor; "he is a brilliant man. But you will have to put him in a cage with seven locks. That's the best place to leave him to draft his engine designs. But he will have to pass his drawings through the bars so that, with luck, he won't be able

to get his hands on the drawings or the engine again!" Well-staffed with engineers as it was, also at management board level, DMG was confident that it could cope with this creative spirit. Ernst Berge remembered Porsche, the youthful prodigy, from his spell in Vienna 20 years earlier. Daimler decided to engage Porsche.

His five-year contract as board member and technical director didn't take effect until the end of April 1923; Porsche's first official board-meeting presence would be on May 4. Nevertheless, in February, Ferdinand Porsche already was ensconced in Stuttgart's Hotel Marquardt and hard at work. He soon arranged for other members of his Austro-Daimler team to join him, including his trusted design engineer, Otto Köhler, and the head of his vehicle running-in department, Alfred Neubauer. He rented a villa at 176 Eduard-Pfeiffer-Strasse for his family until his own new house at 48–50 Feuerbacherweg was ready. The new spacious white villa with its tiled roof was the work of architects

Friedrich Eugen Scholer and Paul Bonatz.

The Bohemian engineer "was welcomed with anything but open arms" at Untertürkheim, wrote Porsche's biographer Peter Müller. Resentment over a man parachuted in at such a high level was only to be expected from senior engineers, especially if they were puffed-up "steam blatherers" of the ilk that Porsche openly despised. His no-nonsense style of direct and personal involvement in the drawing offices, shop floor and test stands was in startling and unnerving contrast to that of Paul Daimler, who preferred to overlook his domain from on high.

A more fundamental phenomenon was also at work. K.B. Hopfinger wrote that Porsche encountered "certain difficulties with the human element in that part of the country, people with whom he was to live and work for almost the remainder of his life. The population around Stuttgart, as in other parts of the province of Württemberg, is mostly Swabian, very God-fearing, hardworking and good-natured people, with a colossal zest for life and a pride in their skill to turn out well-finished goods, yet on the other hand, they show an unmistakable reserve toward strangers who come to work in their midst."

Ferdinand Porsche soon learned just how narrow-minded the Swabians could be. He had his new business cards printed with "Dr. h. c. F. Porsche," as before, only to be told that this wasn't acceptable. A Viennese honorary doctorate was all very well in Austria, he was told by Württemberg's Interior Ministry, but wasn't up to Germany's standards. The cards would have to be reprinted. "Porsche responded with work and performance," wrote a nephew about this petty episode.

There was no shortage of work. In fact, Porsche found himself in the midst of final preparations for the most ambitious racing effort ever undertaken by Daimler, a campaign one of the participants said "cost our company an enormous amount of money." It sent a team of three supercharged, 2-liter, four-cylinder Mercedes to race 500 miles at Indianapolis in America in May of 1923. Running as high as third and finishing eighth and eleventh in the Indy 500, the

Above: The 1934 Audi front-wheel-drive Cabriolet had a 40hp, 1949cc Wanderer engine designed by Ferdinand Porsche. Right: Prof. Porsche at the company offices at Zuffenhausen.

new cars proved their toughness but not their ability to hold a supercharged state of tune. On July 23, the Daimler board decided to suspend its racing activities for that season. It would prepare better for 1924.

Here was a task to Ferdinand Porsche's liking. Probing every aspect of Paul Daimler's four-cylinder design, frequently driving the test cars himself at the age of 48, he dedicated himself to their improvement. After his revisions, including new valve gear akin to his last designs for the Saschas, this twin-cam Mercedes scored the fine victory in the Targa Florio on April 27, 1924, for which the cars are celebrated. Works test driver Christian Werner mastered his car and the field to win both the Targa and Coppa Florio.

This was a stunning success in one of the most respected races of the day. When Werner, Porsche and the red Mercedes returned from Sicily to Stuttgart, they were hailed in the town-hall square as conquering heroes. Following a paean of praise from the Mayor, Porsche was asked to sign Stuttgart's golden book of

high honors. He was also awarded an honorary doctorate by Stuttgart's Technical Institute. Granted "in recognition of his outstanding merit in the field of motor car design and particularly as designer of the winning car in the 1924 Targa Florio," this was the German recognition that Porsche needed. In 1929 he added an honorary Dipl.-Ing. degree from the Württemberg Technical Institute.

In an unusual step that implied continued commitment, early in 1924, Daimler decided to acquire the rights to Porsche's inventions as well. His patent palette was already imposing, from his early electric innovations through his engine and chassis developments at Austro-Daimler. Indeed, it included the valve gear used in the winning Targa Mercedes and was exemplified by the advanced ADM Mixte he'd brought with him to Stuttgart. Thus, on February 21, 1924, the management board decided to buy Porsche's existing patent rights. This provided the engineer with a welcome financial windfall.

His Targa four wasn't Porsche's last word on the subject of the ideal racing car to compete under the 2-liter Grand Prix racing formula. Four powerful and handsome, supercharged, straight-eight-cylinder Mercedes cars that met that criterion were entered for the Italian Grand Prix on October 19, 1924. The imperturbable Christian Werner would drive one and the very fast Count Giulio Masetti another. Alfred Neubauer was assigned a third car and the fourth was handled by English Count Louis Zborowski.

The main opposition in the 60-lap 497-mile race was the strong Alfa Romeo P2 team. Sometime Alfa team member Masetti challenged them with his Mercedes, running second on the first lap and then falling to fourth before retiring. Zborowski managed a pit stop in spite of clutch problems and returned to the fray, but failed to finish his 44th lap. Coming out of the fast Lesmo turn, according to an eyewitness, "the Mercedes suddenly snaked and then spun across the road. The car careered against two posts and ended up against a tree ... facing in the opposite direction from which it had come." Zborowski was thrown from the car and killed in an accident which, for Porsche and Neubauer, evoked distressing memories of Fritz Kuhn at the same track two years earlier.

This was the tragic finale for the only major international race entry made by Porsche's 2-liter, eight-cylinder Mercedes. His eight's advanced power unit had tremendous potential that was only partially realized. In the Daimler tradition, it used fabricated-steel cylinders like its main competitors, Fiat and Alfa Romeo, but it differed from them in retaining the four valves for each cylinder that had worked well for DMG in the past and had been the subject of Porsche's final experiments with the Saschas at Wiener Neustadt. Sodium-cooled valves were inclined in a pent-roof combustion chamber and opened by twin overhead camshafts.

In the development of peak power, Porsche's Roots-supercharged Mercedes eight was outstanding. It produced 170 bhp at 7,000 rpm and was engineered to operate safely to 8,000 rpm, an advance of some 25 percent over accepted racing-engine speeds. Only the French Delage V12 and a handful of centrifugally supercharged American Miller eights surpassed its output under the 2-liter formula that concluded in 1925. Its power curve was very peaky, however, making it hard to start and short on torque. DMG people would attribute this to Porsche's choice of a supercharger that sucked from the carburetor instead of blowing through it. Ultimately this method of supercharging would prove the better solution, but Porsche's embodiment of it was ahead of its time.

More than was customary in other Grand Prix cars, the engine was placed well to the rear in the 2-liter's chassis. Porsche also carried over an innovation of his Saschas by fitting a 25-gallon fuel tank into the space beneath the seats and ahead of the rear axle, where fuel depletion least affected the car's weight distribution. Thus, its main weight masses were concentrated toward the center.

It was then – and remained for more than a decade – Ferdinand Porsche's conviction that such a central grouping of its main masses made a vehicle less likely

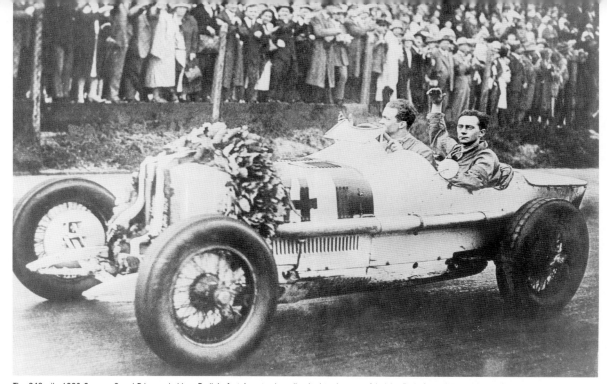

The 243-mile 1926 German Grand Prix was held on Berlin's fast Avus track, well suited to the powerful eight. Rudy Caracciola and Eugen Salzer accepted the crowd's applause for their victory from their garland-decked Mercedes.

to generate the forces in a turn that would act to make one pair of tires or the other break loose from the pavement to slide outward and cause a loss of control. His conception was founded on the assumption that in a racing car, it was better to have such masses as the engine and fuel close to the center instead of dispersing them toward the front and rear.

In the context of the chassis-design parameters of the 1920s, this approach made the Mercedes agile in its cornering, but when one or the other pair of tires did ultimately break away in a corner, the car would yaw very quickly, so quickly in fact that only the best drivers could catch it. Appreciation of this behooved little in the wake of the death of Louis Zborowski. This inevitably led to the first negative nigglings among the DMG management—as Fritz Kuhn's death had at Wiener Neustadt—about the competence of their technical chief.

One driver who was able to take advantage of the agility of Porsche's eight was Rudolf Caracciola,

who would become one of the brightest stars in the Mercedes firmament. On July 11, 1926, he drove one in the German Grand Prix, converted with the addition of a vestigial rear seat into a "sports car." The first race of that name ever held, it was staged on a four-lane toll known as the Avus, running southwest from Berlin toward Pottsdam. Adding connecting loops at each end of the Avus converted the divided highway into a 12.2-mile track for the Grand Prix.

After 243 miles and almost three hours of chaotic competition that started in the dry and continued in pelting rain, before more than 200,000 Berliners, Caracciola crossed the finish line exhausted. He and riding mechanic Eugen Salzer were stunned to learn they had won the first Grand Prix of Germany at the impressive average speed of 83.95 mph (135.10 km/h). It was the finest result for Porsche's eight in the most important German race of the year. It was also fitting celebration after the creation of the Daimler-Benz Aktiengesellschaft a fortnight earlier.

The Artist's Artist

Art Gallery with Bernie Fuchs

Bernie Fuchs in studio, photo courtesy of B. Hacke.

Seldom has an artist enjoyed accolades from his peers as much as illustrator Bernie Fuchs has throughout his long, successful and diverse career. Fuchs has been called the most influential illustrator of the second half of the 20th century.

BY LEIGH DORRINGTON

Left: Painted in 1963, this is Bernie Fuchs' favorite automobile illustration.

W*riting in* Illustration *magazine, David Apatoff quoted Walt Reed,*
the world's foremost authority on illustration art, as saying:

"His pictures are probably more admired – and more
imitated – than those of any current illustrator."

Illustrations for *Sports Illustrated*, 1961.

Most widely known perhaps are his illustrations and covers for publications such as *Sports Illustrated*. His paintings of golf, baseball, yachting, boxing, horse racing – and auto racing – have been widely admired. He is also an exceptional portrait artist, whose subjects have included John F. Kennedy, Martin Luther King and Queen Elizabeth. He is highly regarded as a book illustrator; *Illustration* magazine has devoted an entire issue to his career. Susan Viebrock, who reviewed a 50-year Fuchs retrospective in Telluride, Colo., in 2008, calls Fuchs "a poet painter of everyday life."

What few of Fuchs' many admirers know is that his career began creating illustrations for automakers in Detroit.

Left: Illustration for *Sports Illustrated*, 1961. Above and Below: Oldsmobile advertisements by Fuchs and Ben Jaroslaw, 1958 and 1957.

Above left: Another example of Fuchs' ambitious backgrounds for automobile advertising, 1960. Left: On the scene – Indianapolis 500 pitstop illustration for *Sports Illustrated*, 1961. Above: Advertisement for Mobil, 1958.

YOUNG MAN WITH A HORN

Bernie Fuchs nearly didn't become an artist. He was born in 1932 in O'Fallon, Ill., a small coal-mining town. Jazz was his first love. By the age of six he had already decided he would play with Glenn Miller's band, and as a teenager he jammed with bands in St. Louis. Art classes weren't even offered in his high school. But after losing part of three fingers from his playing hand in an industrial accident, he became an artist. It was an inspired decision.

After graduating from Washington University in St. Louis in 1954, his first job was illustrating backgrounds for automobile advertisements at New Center Studios in Detroit. Less than 10 years later, he was one of the top illustrators in America.

David Apatoff described Bernie Fuchs' early career. "Fuchs worked in a large studio for a boss who promised, 'If you stay with me, I guarantee I will make you the richest illustrator in all of Detroit.' The work was safe and lucrative, but Fuchs knew he was capable of more." Fuchs and other artists formed their own studio called the Art Group. It was soon the busiest studio in Detroit, leading to commissions from New York advertising agencies and publications.

Viebrock wrote, "Fuchs wound up turning the field of commercial illustration on its head." He was named Artist of the Year by the Artists Guild of New York in 1962 at the age of 30 and elected as the youngest member of the Society of Illustrators Hall of Fame in 1975. The United States Sports Academy named him Sport Artist of the Year in 1991, the same year he was commissioned by the Indianapolis Motor Speedway to create a series of paintings for the 75th anniversary of the Indianapolis 500. In 1998, he was commissioned by the U.S. Postal Service to create a set of four commemorative stamps honoring folk musicians.

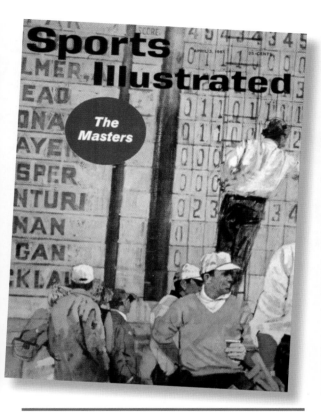

ILLUSTRATION OR FINE ART

Fuchs' work has been praised for the ability to capture the essence or mood of his subjects, be they people, places or events. His commissioned paintings for the Indianapolis Motor Speedway are typical of this ability. In one, depicting the first Indianapolis 500 in 1911, infield spectators in their holiday-best clothes fill the foreground while Ray Harroun in the winning Marmon Wasp passes slower competitors on the dusty track. An American flag flies over the covered grandstand marking the Memorial Day holiday. This painting was selected for the Society of Illustrators Gold Medal in 1992. The second painting in the series features three front-wheel-drive racers from 1935, including Bill Cummings' Boyle Miller Special, Wilbur Shaw's Pirrung-Offy and one of the

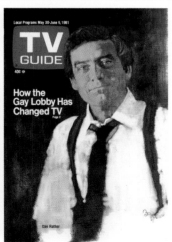

Above left: *Sports Illustrated* cover, 1961. Above: Fuchs painted car advertisements in real-life scenes, 1957. Far left: Illustration for *Lithopinion* magazine, 1970. Left: Portrait of Dan Rather for *TV Guide*, 1981.

Above: Illustration for *ESPN*, 1981. Above right: Pencil sketch of members of Jack Sheldon's band. Right: One of a series of New Orleans jazz portraits for Time-Life books, 1980.

Miller-Ford V8s. Official guests – men only, in the era – line the pit wall in suits, ties and fedoras.

The third painting shows a pivotal moment in Speedway history: A.J. Foyt's George Bignotti pit crew work on Foyt's Offy roadster while other crews lean over the wall to watch as Jim Clark's Lotus-Ford races out of the pits ahead. The year is 1964. Clark's Lotus would be out of the race by lap 47 with a failed suspension, while Foyt would go on to victory in the last roadster to win Indy. The painting captures the poignancy of that moment, when the future hung in the balance. The fourth painting, from a very different angle that emphasized tremendous speed, shows the start of the 1990 race with pole-setter Emerson Fittipaldi and Rick Mears in Penske-Chevrolets already leading Bobby Rahal and eventual race winner Arie Luyendyk in Lola-Chevrolets. Each of the paintings clearly represents an era, a story and a specific moment in history.

A similar painting was created as a foldout cover for the Official Race Program on the 75th anniversary of the Indianapolis 500. The image shows Harroun in the 1911 race-winning Marmon surrounded by multiple-500 winners. The background pictures the old scoring pagoda and the grandstands from 1911, while the Marmon and race champions from eight decades stand on a symbolic brick-paved track.

The Indy series is also typical of the studious attention to detail and composition that characterizes Fuchs' paintings. The object, such as Clark's Lotus, is often toward the bottom of the painting, with the artist favoring "dynamic assymetries" that reflect the challenges of magazine assignments, where a title and copy would have to fit into the painting. His work has been described as the work of an illustrator and an impressionist painter. His work has been compared with that of contemporary fine artists including Robert Motherwell, Robert Rauschenberg and Franz Kline, rejecting "the realistic paintings of predecessors (such as Norman Rockwell) and focusing on broader qualities of abstract design and composition."

Illustration for *Sports Illustrated*, 1961.

Fuchs represents a bridge between two significant eras of American art. The artists who most influenced his early work, he says, were Coby Whitmore, Al Parker, Joe DeMers and Austin Briggs. As a young man, he became a contemporary of Norman Rockwell when both worked on the faculty of the Famous Artists School. He stood for a faculty portrait with Rockwell and another giant of illustra-

Above: One in a series to commemorate the 75th anniversary of the Indianapolis 500, 1991. Above right: Franz Klammer's Gold Run, in the collection of the Mountain Village Conference Center in Telluride, CO. Right: An Indianapolis 500 pitstop illustration for *Sports Illustrated*, 1961.

tion and automotive art, Peter Helck. With his own generation, he was one of the founding members of the influential Illustrators Workshop, which presented art seminars worldwide.

Fuchs is at all times gracious, forthcoming and describes himself simply. "I'm basically an illustrator." He might also describe himself as a very fortunate individual; just a year out of art school he was working in Detroit, had a car and was ready to marry his home-town sweetheart, Babe Hesse, who also happened to be the mayor's daughter from O'Fallon. They've been married for more than 50 years and have raised three children: Cindy, Derek and Ellise, all working in creative professions but none as artists.

His arrival in Detroit was the stuff of the American Dream. While still at Washington University, he had the opportunity to work in the St. Louis studio of Bob Cassell, who became a mentor and made it clear that Fuchs would have a full-time job as soon as he graduated. But shortly before graduation, a Washington University alumnus who was working in Detroit stopped by the school. He took one look at Fuchs' work and the work of a fellow student, Bob Whitesett, and told them both they could be working in Detroit. Fuchs and Whitesett took their portfolios to Detroit during spring break of their senior year. They had one appointment, at LaDriere studios, which did work for Cadillac and other automakers. They both left with job offers, but staffers at LaDriere also gave them names of other studios they should visit. They received offers from every one.

The most significant, however, was the New Center Studios of Art Greenwald. Fuchs and Whitesett were planning to visit one more studio, in Chicago, on their way back to St. Louis. But Greenwald audaciously told them, "Leave your portfolios here. The day you graduate, you'll have a job here on the board at $5,000 a year." In addition to the money and the promise of full-time work, "on the board" meant the status and a steady flow of work typically reserved for more experienced illustrators. Most new hires started out in the bullpen.

Illustration for AMF.

Left: "Perfect Afternoon." Above: Legends of American Music Series, U.S. Postal Service, 1998. Below: Illustration from the book *Ride Like the Wind*, 2004, which Fuchs also wrote.

Fuchs started in Detroit and immediately began pushing the boundaries of the entire illustration field. His early work included assignments for Oldsmobile, GMC trucks, Pontiac and Cadillac. Dick Meissner worked with Fuchs at New Center and told David Aptatoff, "Nobody in Detroit was painting like Bernie was. There were a few people in New York who were experimenting along those lines, such as Austin Briggs. But in Detroit, Bernie's art really stood out."

Automobile illustrators worked in teams, one to illustrate the background and a technical illustrator who painted the car. Fuchs was fortunate to work with Ben Jaroslaw at New Center. Jaroslaw was 10 years older and a WWII veteran, and he became a mentor. He said of Fuchs, "Bernie was a painter's painter, one of the greatest illustrators I have ever seen. He would always pick exactly the right pose for his figures. He had a gift that nobody else did."

Not everyone was as complimentary, but his critics were few. Art directors and editors who were not open to

change were resistant. Fuchs and others formed the Art Group as a way to get into the New York art market.

While he was still working in Detroit, Fuchs discovered another opportunity that would have an important effect on the rest of his career – and his life. The field of magazine illustration was one in which artists such as Norman Rockwell, Peter Helck, Coby Whitmore and Austin Briggs dominated. The industry was centered in New York, and many of the artists lived in the small town of Westport, Conn., an easy train ride from the city. By the late 1950s, publications providing steady work for illustrations accompanying their stories included women's magazines such as *McCall's*, *Redbook* and *Ladies' Home Journal*. Fuchs' work was ideally suited to the genre. In Detroit, he was already widely imitated for the figures he placed in car ads, as well as his experimentation with backgrounds and settings. In New York, he found a new group of art directors who readily embraced his innovative style.

Left: Portrait of John F. Kennedy, originally intended for *TV Guide*. Top: Book illustration for *Ragtime Tumpie*, 1989. Above: Illustration for *Reader's Digest*.

Below left: Oscar Charleston, for *Sports Illustrated*, 2005. Above left: A typical Fuchs illustration for *McCall's*, 1960-63. Above right: One in a series to commemorate the 75th running of the Indianapolis 500, 1991.

STORY ILLUSTRATIONS

Bernie Fuchs' first story illustration for *McCall's* was done in 1959, while he was still in Detroit. He quickly recognized that this field, as well as ongoing assignments for ad agencies, many of which were also in New York, was his future. At the urging of a Detroit friend, Tully Rector, a commercial producer who had moved to New York, Fuchs and Babe made the move in 1959 as well, settling in Westport.

Speaking with the author 50 years later, he marvels at how easily he was accepted into the company of the same artists who had been his inspiration. "In Detroit, everyone was a competitor. We knew who the guys were in other studios, but we rarely met them. They were the competition. In New York, there was none of that." Bernie Burroughs, a well-known fashion illustrator, and Austin Briggs became two of his first friends in Westport. Briggs introduced Fuchs to Al Dorne, president of the Famous Artists School, and Dorne introduced Fuchs to Norman Rockwell over lunch in New York.

The artist also met illustrators Joe Bowler, Al Parker and Coby Whitmore in New York and became a friend. Fuchs told David Apatoff that he "could not believe that three of his heroes had accepted him into their ranks" and described how, the same day he met all three, the four illustrators "took a long stroll down 3rd Avenue together, talking and looking in the old shop windows for curios and props to use in their illustrations."

"Bernie hit his stride just as the women's magazines were hitting theirs. A new generation of art directors was taking control of these magazines. Herb Mayes, Otto Storch and other art directors of vision began to recognize new potential for these magazines. They began to plan double page spreads with unconventional layouts and typography. Most importantly, they gave a longer leash to a whole generation of new illustrators, and Bernie was foremost among them."

His work was prolific, and *Sports Illustrated* was soon added to the list of magazines commissioning his work. Art director Dick Gangel was another casual introduction who quickly became a significant patron. Fuchs was soon creating illustrations for

Sports Illustrated to accompany stories that eventually included virtually all of the major sporting events in the world. His first assignment for auto racing was the 1961 Indianapolis 500, where he created a series of illustrations from the pits, showing an insider's view of the event – work that would later become the domain of photographers. He continued to work with *Sports Illustrated* and Gangel for more than 25 years, even after Gangel's retirement.

Automobiles were an unexpected and ongoing element in the artist's work, simply because he enjoyed automobiles and still does. His story illustrations for women's magazines and other publications frequently included automobiles either as an element of the story or as part of the background. His first sports car, a 1958 Porsche Cabriolet, appeared in his illustrations, as did Rector's Mercedes-Benz 300SL Gullwing and Rector's wife Gloria who frequently provided a model for his figures.

One of his story illustrations that included automobiles was done for *Redbook*. "It's of a lady sitting in the back seat of a Duesenberg, and I did it during the period when I was using acrylics," Fuchs said. "It became quite well known and it made the Illustrators Show. I've seen a couple of guys who've copied it – the composition, everything. It is my favorite car painting."

THE POST–ILLUSTRATION ERA

As for illustration today, Fuchs says, "There's so much digital (art) going on, I don't know where illustrators are getting their work. And yet, the Society of Illustrators in New York has their annual show and they're packed with illustrations. And it's quite good."

Fuchs considers children's book illustration as "probably the greatest field to get into." His own career has taken him in this direction, and he also has both written and illustrated a book on the Pony Express. "And they're still doing a lot of illustration in the movie industry."

Asked if he works solely in the fine art and print market, he replies with a simple no. Just as innovation has always defined Fuchs' work, he continues to redefine himself. At age 76, he has just completed the Telluride 50-year retrospective of his work. The oldest piece in the exhibition was a 1958 Oldsmobile painted for an advertisement when he worked in Detroit. The newest pieces show altogether new directions for those familiar with his earlier work.

"I paint mostly Italian scenes for the galleries because we go over there every year," he said. One of their daughters has married in Italy and is raising a family there. "We just love Italy, and I do all kinds of paintings of Italy – courtyards, street scenes, buildings. It keeps my interest going."

He talks about other recent projects, including a cover for the *Eddie Bauer* Christmas catalog and paintings, including a program cover and prints, for the AT&T Pebble Beach golf tournament in 2010. He is also developing ideas for an illustrated children's version of Jack London's classic story *White Fang*.

Above and left: Roman courtyard mystery – the car that wasn't there.

Automobiles continue to find their way into his paintings, often in unexpected places. "Courtyards and streets in Italy are where you see cars," he said, although "my wife, Babe, keeps telling me the cars don't belong in the paintings." He relates a humorous experience with one recent painting that seems to speak volumes about him and Babe, who have shared a remarkable life together.

"I had painted a Roman courtyard, projecting a photo onto the canvas. There was a car in the

Book cover and two of the many interior illustrations from the book *Ride Like the Wind*, 2004. Fuchs also authored this story about the Pony Express.

Ride Like the Wind
A TALE OF THE PONY EXPRESS
by Bernie Fuchs

photograph. Babe saw it and said, 'You're not putting the car in the painting, are you?' The next day I walked into my studio and, where the car would have been, there was a post-it note that said 'No Parking.' I always shoot with slides and Babe always shoots with film, so I thought I'd get back at her. The painting was almost finished, but I painted a car into the courtyard and took a picture of the painting on her camera. After I took the picture, I wiped away the car. When she picked up her film after having it developed, she checked the prints in the store as she always does. She saw the picture with the car in it and let out a scream in the photo store. She came into my studio, looked at the painting – with no car – and looked puzzled. I said, 'Well, it wasn't a "No Parking" sign; it was a "15-Minute Parking" sign. The car left.'"

GIVING BACK

This kind of easy humor seems typical of Bernie Fuchs, as well as an abiding appreciation for those who influenced and encouraged him. He shares his knowledge, his insights and his interests in the same easy way. He is an entertaining lunch companion, asking frequently, "I'm not boring you with all this, am I?" As if he possibly could.

Fuchs still appears to be surprisingly young for someone who has accomplished so much. He is constantly busy and frequently plays golf. He drives a 1984 Porsche Carrera around Westport, his sixth Porsche. "I never thought I would keep a car for so long, but my son won't let me sell it. He says it's his. But his wife says it's hers!"

One has the feeling that, like Fuchs' lifetime of work, the Porsche will be enjoyed for a very long time. AQ

More of Bernie Fuchs work can be seen online at
www.telluridegallery.com

Below Left: Bernie and his wife Babe, photo courtesy of Herb Weitman. Above: Portrait of Bernie's boyhood hero, Jackie Robinson. Below: Editorial Illustration for *Sports Illustrated*.

IT'S GOOD TO BE GREEN

The Hybri

Colonel Edward Howland Robinson Green made his money the old-fashioned way – he inherited it. That's not to say that life was easy for Green. His personality contrasted with his mother's (a miserly woman named the "Witch of Wall Street"), and his life was marked with continuous ailments, including an amputated leg when just a young man. But thanks to his great wealth, and also because of his physical limitations, Col. Green struck out for automotive innovation, including something of rising interest today, a gas-electric hybrid engine.

BY BILL ROTHERMEL
PHOTOGRAPHY BY DENIS TANNEY

Cars of Col. Edward H.R. Green

Known as Ned by his friends, Col. Green was born in England on Aug. 22, 1868, the only son of Henrietta "Hetty" Howland Robinson Green and Edward H. Green. A sister, Henrietta Sylvia Ann Howland Robinson Green, was born two years later. Hetty was born in New Bedford, Mass., in 1834, and when she and Edward married in 1867, he was the United States Consul General in Manila. Hetty, too, was a woman of inherited wealth. Over time, thanks to both shrewdness and keen insight into financial matters, she added substantially to her holdings. Edward, too, made a great deal of money in the silk trade, but

where Ned was born. They stayed in London at the Langham Hotel for eight years until returning to the United States. Edward's hometown of Bellows Falls, Vt., became home for the Green family, and young Sylvia and Ned attended private school there at the Immanuel Episcopal Church. By 1881, however, Hetty and Edward had separated. Hetty spent a great deal of time in New York City managing her fortune, moving from one flat to another to avoid paying state taxes. She trusted no one and took it upon herself to oversee her ever-increasing portfolio of stocks, bonds and real estate.

age of 21. The amputation later would have a profound effect on both Ned and his interest in the operation of a modern automobile.

Ned attended Fordham University to study law, but he didn't graduate. Hetty put him to work as the foreman of a section gang on the Connecticut River Railroad in Vermont at a salary of $45 a month. Ned learned all about railroad construction from the ground up, including how to run a locomotive. In 1890, Hetty sent her son to Chicago to manage her extensive real estate holdings; he spent two years there. While in Chicago, he met Mabel Harlow, a showgirl who was

Above and right: Col. Green was deeply interested in early electronics, proved out by his curiosity with electric-motor automobiles. Here, Col. Green is seen on his estate, driving his Automatic Electric roadster, circa 1921.

lost most of his fortune on Wall Street prior to his death in 1902.

Hetty was accused of forging her Aunt Sylvia's will, prompting Hetty and Edward to move to England,

At the age of 12, young Ned was involved in a sledding accident in which his left knee was seriously injured. He developed osteomyelitis, which was quite painful, resulting in amputation above his knee at the

neither accepted by Hetty nor New England society. Ned spent the rest of his life with Mabel, but waited to marry her until after the death of his mother.

By 1892, Ned had left Chicago, having been sent to Texas by his mother to buy the Texas Midland Railroad at a foreclosure sale. At the age of 24, he became the youngest president of a railroad in the United States. Green became involved in politics in 1894 and by 1896, he had been elected Texas State Chairman of the Republican Party. In appreciation of Green's three

Above: Green's first Rauch & Lang automobile, a roadster. The unusual device mounted on the rear (right) was for his two dogs, of which he was very fond. This is the vehicle that is presumed scrapped.

terms of service as State Chair, the governor awarded him with the honorary title of "Colonel." He was also the first man in Texas to own a horseless carriage, purchasing a two-cylinder automobile made by the Moon Buggy Company of St. Louis, Mo., in 1899. With great sadness, Green left Texas, moving to New York City in 1911, taking with him both Mabel and his personal secretary Walter Marshall, to more closely manage the family holdings.

Hetty was considered to be the world's wealthiest woman as early as 1900, and she was unceremoniously awarded the title "Witch of Wall Street." She would also earned the distinction of being known as the "Greatest Miser" in the *Guinness Book of World Records*, which noted, "If meanness is measurable as a ratio between expendable assets and expenditure, then Henrietta Howland Green who kept a balance of more than $31,400,00 in one bank alone, was the all-time world champion. She was so stingy that her son had to have his leg amputated because of the delay in finding a free medical clinic. She lived off cold oatmeal because she was too thrifty to heat it, and died of apoplexy in an argument over the virtues of skim milk." (Note: Green biographer Barbara Bedell Fortin maintains that the statement, "She was so stingy that her son had to have his leg amputated because of the delay in finding a free medical clinic," is, in fact, not true). At the time of her death in 1916, Hetty's estate was valued at more than $100 million, the bulk of which was passed directly to son Ned and his sister Sylvia. Ned added to the fortune his mother made, though, unlike her, he enjoyed spending it as much as he enjoyed making it.

Enjoying "The Good Life"

Ned and Mabel married in 1917 and spent their honeymoon cruising aboard their yacht, the *United States*, including a visit to Buzzard's Bay, anchoring off Round Hill, Mass. Two years later, the couple began building a mansion at Round Hill, the property left to him by his mother, with construction completed some two years later. Ned and Mabel called the estate home for the next 14 years, until his death in 1936.

Unlike his penny-pinching mother, Ned, and Mabel, lived the "good life." In addition to the lavish home at Round Hill, the couple wintered at their Star Island, Fla., estate, returning to Round Hill on July 1 each year. Ned was quite philanthropic, but wasn't one to talk of his charitable contributions, which were numerous. He preferred to give privately to avoid the thousands of requests that ultimately appeared after a donation was made public. He invited MIT scientists to open a laboratory for research projects in the areas of radio communication, aircraft navigation, high voltage and meteorology, and supplied the cash for research, buildings and housing on his Round Hill estate.

During the Colonel's years at Round Hill, his health was anything but excellent. He suffered from numerous ailments, such as arthritis, anemia and rheumatism, as well as numerous problems with both legs. Despite his ill health, his mind remained sharp, and he continued to be interested in new technology and offered financial help to advance it. But for all his wealth, Green lacked the simplest of abilities afforded ordinary men – the physical range of movement enabling him to operate a modern automobile. The limited flexibility of his artificial leg made entry and exit from con-

ventional cars difficult. In 1921, Green purchased an obscure Automatic Electric roadster, with a top speed of 18mph, for $1,200. Fitted with hand controls, the limited-range electric enabled Green to traverse the grounds of his vast Massachusetts estate, but it failed to fulfill his desire for a modern automobile.

Exactly what sparked the Green's interest in a gas-electric automobile isn't known, but it's possible that it stemmed from his substantial holdings of General Electric stock, and his personal association with the members of its board of directors. That, and Green's willingness and financial wherewithal to underwrite the entire cost, was, no doubt, more than sufficient to get the project underway. GE had the technology available in its existing line of commercial electric drives; the difficulty was in adapting it to a modern automobile chassis. Also, a "no-clutch" car had existed before, most notably the Owen Magnetic, based on the work of Justus B. Entz of Philadelphia, chief electrical engineer of the Electric Storage Battery

Company, makers of Exide Batteries. Author Stuart W. Wells (*Automobile Quarterly Vol. 36, No. 3*) in his article entitled "Car of a Thousand Speeds: The Entz System and Owen Magnetic," wrote: "In the 1890s, J.B. Entz experimented with an electric transmission which, simply put, was basically a motor/generator. A gasoline engine turned a magnetic clutch-generator built integrally with the driveshaft, which produced electric current when it slipped to power an electric motor, also on a common shaft, that helped propel the car. Although Mr. Entz was developing the Entz system in the 1890s, he could almost have passed off as a man of the 1990s. He promoted his hybrid gasoline-electric design and vigorously sought manufacturers who could put his concept into production vehicles. He applied for a patent, but, unfortunately, the 1898 working example of his automobile came to a spectacular – though ignominious – end after an electric arc melted a hole through the gas tank and the car went up in flames."

Entz continued to refine his product and introduced his Entz Six at the January 1914 New York Automobile Show. Rather than entering series production, the Entz electric transmission was instead fitted to the new Owen Magnetic debuting at the New York Automobile Show in January 1915. The car was sponsored by the R.M. Owen Company, which was itself an outgrowth of the R.M Owen Carpet Cleaning and Rug Manufacturing Company of Cleveland, Ohio. Brothers Raymond and Ralph began their foray into the motorized vehicle business in 1899 by fitting an 8hp engine of their own design onto a motor wagon for the delivery of their goods. The brothers had been working on refining the Entz principles in New York beginning in 1912, the same year that Walter C. Baker (Baker Electric), also of Cleveland, had secured the Entz patents.

The first Owen Magnetics were built in New York City under license from Baker, with the company moving to Cleveland, Ohio, in 1915. Cleveland was also home to Baker Electric, which had just merged with competitor Rauch & Lang. The merged company decided to focus its attention on the Owen Magnetic, in part due to the declining interest in electric cars. Owen Magnetics were luxurious and expensive with with prices ranging from $3,000 upwards of $6,500, this at a time when a Model T cost as little as $440. The car attracted a wealthy clientele, but production declined with Baker R&L turning to military work. Owen Magnetic discontinued production in mid-1919 when Raymond Owen moved the company to Wilkes Barre, Penn., where production later resumed. The revival was short lived, as Owen Magnetic fell into receivership, closing its doors in November 1921; the complicated and expensive electric transmission had proven both impractical to manufacture and market. The Entz Motors Patents Corp. dissolved by 1923, and Justus Entz, working out of an office in New Rochelle, N.Y., kept busy with consulting work for automotive electrical equipment manufacturers. Raymond Owen flourished all the while, continuing to build his new company, the Owen-Dyneto Electric Corp., in Syracuse.

Green was so impressed with his first Rauch & Lang that he purchased another, this one a brougham. This car exists today, unrestored and in pieces.

Above: The Rauch & Lang brougham. Below: The Green estate consisted of the mansion and three small buildings to the left of it: a combination laundry and garage (nearest to the mansion), a transformer house and another garage. None of the smaller buildings exist today.

line and electric Rauch & Lang taxicabs began in 1922 in a new facility in Chicopee Falls, Mass., next door to the existing factory. Stevens-Duryea quickly found itself in receivership and was again reorganized in 1923 under a syndicate headed by Raymond M. Owen, formerly of Owen Magnetic and holder of the Entz patents. Owen purchased the company for $450,000 in 1923, and long-time associate Robert W. Stanley took over as head of Rauch & Lang. Raymond's brother Ralph Owen became general manager of the newly organized Stevens-Duryea Motors, Inc. The Stevens-Duryea was an exceedingly expensive and outdated car, with prices approaching $10,000. As such, only a few were built, and Stevens-Duryea would produced its last car in 1926.

The Rauch & Lang division found itself struggling, too, as the electric taxicabs didn't sell well; only a smattering of electric vehicles were produced. By 1924, the Chicopee Falls plant was offered for sale in an effort to pay tax claims, yet an extension was

THE RAUCH & LANG APPROACH

Another player in this effort to build a hybrid car was Rauch & Lang, Inc. Beginning life as the Rauch & Lang Carriage Company, it was first incorporated in Cleveland, Ohio, in 1884. It was founded by partners Jacob Rauch, a German immigrant who had set up shop in 1853 as a blacksmith and wagon repairer, later expanding into wagon building, and Charles E.J. Lang, a Cleveland real estate magnate. By the turn of the century, R&L carriages were among the most expensive and best known in the area. The company produced its first electric car in 1905, and then merged with the Baker Motor Vehicle Company in 1915 as stated earlier. The resulting company was known as the Baker R&L Company, though it became popularly known, as did its cars, as Baker-Raulang, a name the company never officially adopted. The Baker name had disappeared by 1916, with only Rauch & Langs produced thereafter.

By January 1920, the electric car had largely fallen out of favor, and the Rauch & Lang division was purchased by Stevens-Duryea. The Stevens-Duryea brand had been revived in July 1919, courtesy of Ray S. Deering and several other Stevens-Duryea alumni, after the company ceased production in June 1915. Deering and team updated the company's six-cylinder engine, along with other refinements. Production of both gaso-

granted and the company continued to survive on a shoestring. Late in 1928, half of the factory was leased to the Moth Aircraft Corporation, with passenger-car production coming to an end later that year. While commercial-vehicle production continued, the Wall Street crash in 1929 precluded any presumptions of resuming car production. However, shortly before the crash in August 1929, C.D. Wagoner of General

Electric in Schenectady, N.Y., issued a memo to his company's publicity department in which he advised of "a new type of pleasure automobile ... one impossible to stall and impossible to start with a jerk ... all that is required to get underway is to step on the gas." Wagoner further explained that the 70hp motor combined with a special gearless electric transmission would provide a unique driving experience and was the result of efforts between General Electric Co. and Rauch & Lang, Inc.

CUSTOMIZED FOR GREEN

With this knowledge of electric motors and their makers, Green purchased a 1929 Stearns-Knight Model M-6-80 cabriolet roadster for $2,195, and he had it delivered to Rauch &

Lang in Chicopee Falls for conversion to gas-electric operation. Why a Stearns-Knight? The decision was likely influenced by the characteristically quiet sleeve-valve engine and the high-quality construction for which the company was well known. Rauch & Lang, with its nearby location, as well as a workforce familiar with electric transmissions and skilled in body-building, was also a logical choice. In addition, the Colonel had previously owned a 1914 Rauch & Lang Electric (which today resides in the collection of the Owls Head Transportation Museum in Owls Head, Maine).

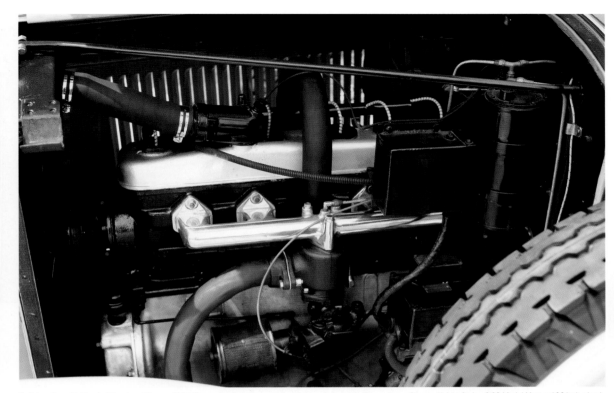

the rear. Rauch & Lang, too, was pleased, revealing in the *Springfield Union* that it would soon begin limited production of the car.

The second car was delivered to Green's Round Hill estate in October 1929. Not the limousine body previously reported, it was a 126-inch-wheelbase Stearns-Knight chassis with six-cylinder engine. Fitted with a custom body likely fashioned by Rauch & Lang, the car was an unusual high-topped brougham coach with china closet carrosserie similar to electric cars of the prior decade. Mechanically, it was a twin to the previous car, though it lacked the vacuum-assisted brakes of its predecessor and is equipped with a conventional

Collaboration with Rauch & Lang and Stearns-Knight to produce hybrid-powered vehicles culminated in this sedan, a Stearns-Knight Series 6-80 Model M on a 126-inch wheelbase chassis, built in late-1929 and mated to a Willys-Knight 66A six-cylinder. The 255cid engine was rated at 70 hp at 3200 rpm, the power for all 6-80 Stearns-Knights.

Aside from its double-height windshield, nearly seven feet high, enabling Green to literally walk into the car, and its corresponding tent-like convertible top, the real differences were out of sight, underneath the car.

In combination with the sleeve-valve, Knight, six-cylinder engine, a variable-speed, variable-voltage GE generator was mounted directly to the engine's flywheel in place of the clutch's and manual transmission's usual location. It was then connected via a differential coupling to an electric motor having the same characteristics as the generator. A short driveshaft coupled the system to the car's worm-drive rear axle. Because the electric motor turned at a much higher speed than the gasoline engine, the rear axle ratio was changed from 4.438:1 to 8.25:1, which enabled a top speed of 40 mph. GE claimed that speeds similar

to a conventional gas-powered automobile could be achieved by replacing the rear-end gearset. Heavy-duty electric cables extended from the generator to a controller mounted on the car's wooden firewall (necessary to eliminate voltage loss and possible electric shocks) and back to the electric motor. The car was fitted with brake and accelerator pedals, but, prior to delivery, a hand-operated, Westinghouse, braking unit was installed, thereby eliminating the brake pedal and easing operation for Green.

According to contemporary news reports, Green "insisted upon taking the wheel himself and for the first time in his life, drove a gasoline-powered automobile." He was so pleased that he ordered a second vehicle with a limousine body and a third, an open-touring car with an elevated driver's seat mounted in

floor-mounted brake pedal. The car is said to have been housed at Green's Florida estate for seasonal use.

The third car was the most conventional in appearance. It was built in late-1928, though it is registered as a 1930. The sedan, a Stearns-Knight Series 6-80 Model M 126-inch wheelbase chassis, is mated to a Willys-Knight 66A six-cylinder. The 255cid engine was rated at 70 hp at 3200 rpm, the power for all 6-80 Stearns-Knights. Though all chassis were assembled in a Willys-Overland plant, they were upgraded to Stearns standards. It's thought that the body was built by Rauch & Lang (Raulang) because the company supplied seven-passenger bodies for Stearns-Knight during 1928-29. One might conclude that this was the preproduction prototype because it's equipped with a conventional body. The two previous cars were built specifically to accommodate Green, with tall passenger compartments in order for him to enter and exit comfortably; this car was not. Further evidence to this effect is the inventory of Green's cars dated Nov. 12, 1931, which includes the roadster and brougham vehicles with no mention of this conventional sedan.

The car was capable of 65 mph and delivered 14 mpg, comparable to a conventional model of the same make, though a comfortable cruising speed was about 50 mph. Thanks to the conversion process, acceleration is leisurely, as the hybrid hardware added 1,300 pounds compared to the non-gasoline-electric model. According to previous owner Bill Mastics, "The car actually floats away from a stop and can be compared to a steam car in its sensation of movements. There is a slight, perhaps half-a-second delay while the motor builds up revolutions to create the electric current needed to put the car in action. Behind the wheel, when you start out you can literally feel the great amount of power building up as the gasoline engine is accelerated. At idle speeds there is not enough current being generated to move the car but as the engine speeds up an automatic control kicks in to start the car moving. To slow down, you simply let up on the gas pedal." With no clutch pedal, the operator would select neutral, reverse, or two forward speeds from an instrument panel-mounted push-pull knob. "To reverse the car, there is a small lever on the dash which actuates a reversing switch under the hood that reverses the flow of electric current to the big electric drive motor," Mastics said.

It's reported that Green invested $1 million of his own money on the technology necessary to build his three cars. Unfortunately, the stock market crashed, Stearns-Knight officially ended production of cars on Dec. 20, 1929, and Col. Green would have his three cars with no need for more. Without his financial backing, R&L would throw in the towel as well, and the unusual collaboration would be relegated to the history books.

Though all Stearns-Knight chassis were assembled in a Willys-Overland plant, they were upgraded to Stearns standards. It's thought that the body of this story's color-photographed car was built by Rauch & Lang (Raulang), as the company supplied seven-passenger bodies for Stearns-Knight during 1928-29.

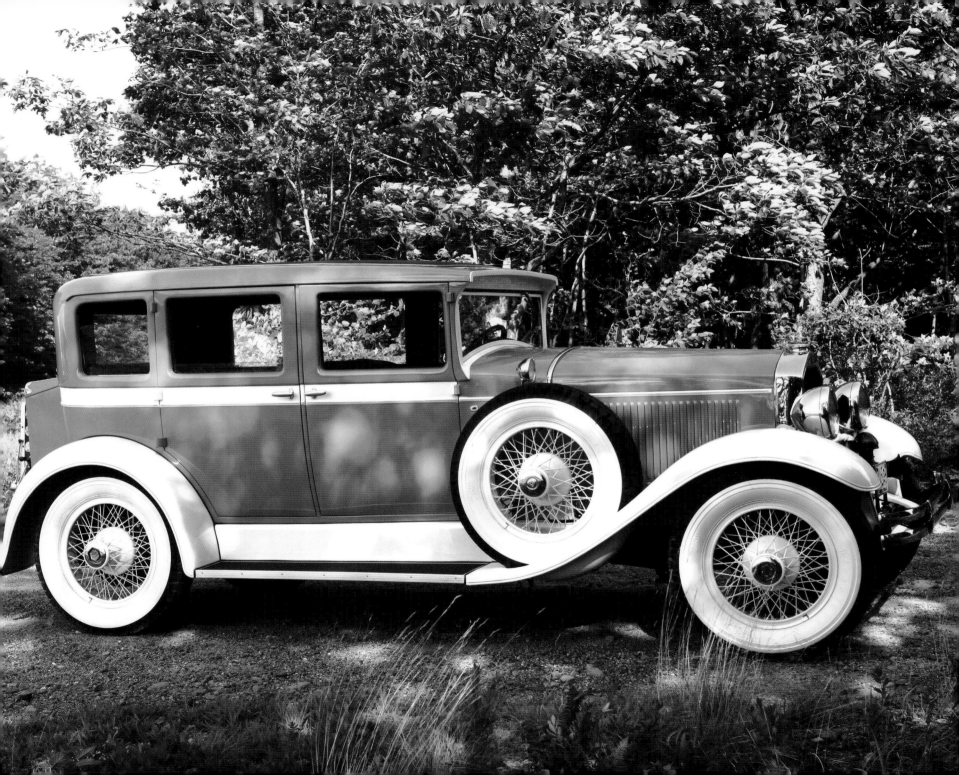

Green's model-year 1930 Stearns-Knight was capable of 65 mph and delivered 14 mpg, with a comfortable cruising speed of about 50 mph. Acceleration is leisurely thanks to the hybrid hardware that added 1,300 pounds compared to the non-gasoline-electric model. The car is now owned by Jack Rich Sr. of Pottsville, Pa.

THE CARS TODAY

The Colonel kept all three cars at Round Hill until has death in 1936 at the age of 68. The first car is presumed to have been scrapped sometime thereafter. The second vehicle, the high-topped brougham, went through a succession of owners after being set outside in a Massachusetts field left to rot away. In 2008, it was sold by the estate of John R. Rich of New York (in pieces) to John W. Rich Sr. of Pottsville, Penn. The third car, the handsome sedan shown in color on these pages, was also purchased by Rich in December 2007 from the Al Wiseman Collection in Tarpon Springs, Fla. It resides in restored condition in Rich's museum in Frackville, Pa.

Without question, the words "hybrid car" and "eco-friendly" are buzz words of our times and no doubt recent entries to the pages of Merriam-Webster. It's fashionable to be "green," and automobile manufacturers have wisely seized upon this opportunity. This development is not unlike the early days of the automobile, when steam, electric and internal combustion engines competed for honors as the definitive choice of propulsion among motorists. Other engine types, albeit in small numbers, attempted to gain a foothold in the burgeoning automotive marketplace as well. Among those were fledging hybrids, though, unlike today, gas mileage and efficiency were not necessarily the reasons for their existence.

Yet, similar to today, most of the players in those early days were linked to one another through various relationships. Who would have thought that three cars, courtesy of a man named Green, could have played such an important part in the development of the hybrid automobile? **AQ**

A Züst for Life

THE STORY OF THE ZÜST GREAT RACE CAR

Six cars started in the Great Race from New York to Paris in 1908, but only three crossed the finish line. These cars were a Thomas Flyer from America, which finished first; a Protos from Germany, which finished second; a De Dion; a Moto Bloc; a Sizaire-Naudin from France; and a short-wheel-base, 28/45hp model manufactured by the Züst Company of Milan, Italy, which finished third. It is the latter that we now scrutinize, a model — and, in fact, a company — that has received surprisingly scant historical mention.

BY BARRY MARTIN PATCHETT

Even before the 1908 Great Race, Züst automobiles had a successful racing history, with good showings in the Coppa d'Oro, the 1907 Targa Florio and other events. Züst initially engaged the Marquis Boschi to drive the Great Race car.

Roberto Züst, the Swiss-born company founder, died in 1897 and left the company to his sons, Arturo, Bruno, Otto, Roberto and Silvio. There was a factory in Milan and a machine tool company and a foundry in Intra when experiments with automobiles began in about 1900. Production of automobiles began in 1905 at Milan with two models, the 28/45 hp 7.4-liter car and a 40/50 hp 11.3-liter car; both were large and expensive automobiles.

Züst cars had been introduced to the United States in January 1906 and first entered in local competition on Long Island by Raymond Healy in June of that year. Healy was a partner in the Healy Leather Tire Company of 88-90 Gold Street, New York City. R. Bertelli & Co. of 144 West 39th Street, New York, was the sole importer and Paul de la Chesnaye the only selling agent. The minimal bodywork on the Great Race car was by Schieppati of Milan.

The Great Race Züst left Milan for the 890-km (553-mile) journey to Paris by road with Antonio Scarfoglio, Emilio (aka Giulio) Sirtori and Heinrich (aka Henry or Henri) Haaga aboard. A photo shows it in Milan in front of the Züst building sans mudguards. It was erroneously described, one of many times, as a "Brixia-Züst," an identity problem surrounding the car that survives to this day. A branch company was started in 1906 in Brescia to produce smaller, less-expensive models, but the 28/45 model was never made in Brescia, only in Milan. Even family members made incorrect statements about the race car. For example, the wife of Roberto Züst, son of the founder, mistakenly said that the original car is now in a museum in Turin. There is a Züst in the Museo dell' Auto, but that car is a smaller 1908 10 hp Brixia-Züst and not a racing car. Likewise, over the years, errors have cropped up in numerous sources. T.R. Nicholson went as far as stating, "New York-Paris material is very thin on the ground," in contrast to the well-documented Pekin to Paris event the year before, and "sources as a whole … are few, and often sketchy or patchy, or both … some are confusing and wildly contradictory." The author hopes this article will eliminate some of this confusion.

banquet in San Jose on April 3, the Züst arrived in San Francisco. It was shipped to Seattle with the De Dion on the *City of Puebla* of the Pacific Coast Steamship Company on April 10. The Züst, after completing 4,836 driven miles, left Seattle for Japan with the De Dion on the *Aki Maru* of the NYK Line (Nippon Yusen Kaisha K.K). The shipment of the car was apparently against the wishes of Züst in Italy, and Sirtori had his contract canceled.

The sensational news in May was that the Züst Company withdrew the car from the race and recalled Sirtori to Italy. The withdrawal was denied in early June, as the company sent a Russian nobleman, Baron Scheinvogel, to take over the car and replace Sirtori. Scheinvogel allegedly purchased the car and joined the race in Manchuria. The car arrived in Berlin on Sept. 6 and Paris on Sept. 17, long after the winning Thomas Flyer and the only other finisher, the Protos.

Soon after crossing the finish line, the Baron Scheinvogel vanished, and Scarfoglio left the next

Opposite: As with the Züst company's passenger vehicles, its trucks were large. Above: The 1908 Great Race Züst in Le Havre, with mudguards, just prior to shipment to New York. Right: The Great Race Züst entering Paris, with headlamps and a sidelamp missing. Also missing are the mudguards and folding canvas top.

The Züst arrived in Paris on Jan. 27, 1908, to a tumultuous welcome. The Züst, now with mudguards, then drove the 220 kilometers, approximately 137 miles, to Le Havre with the French entrants and left for New York on Feb. 1 on the steamer *La Lorraine* of the Compagnie Générale Transatlantique (French Line). Mario (Marco) Conti, a driver of Züst racing cars, and a Dr. von Mueller (aka Vollmoeller) accompanied Scarfoglio, Sirtori and Haaga. The French Line has no record of the identity of the cars. Alberto Pirelli represented the car in America and supplied tires for it.

The cars arrived in New York on Feb. 8, with the Marquis Boschi notably absent. The crew was comprised of the journalist Scarfoglio, engineer-driver Sirtori and the mechanic, Haaga. The cars embarked on a trial run to Dobbs Ferry, and crews were hosted to a sumptuous dinner by the Italian Club on West 16th Street. Some cars were garaged in the 12-story Automobile Club of America building at 753 Fifth

Avenue, while the Züst was kept in the company garage at 144 West 39th Street. The car was painted gray, with the green, white and red of the Italian flag on the hood. "Züst" was painted in large red letters on the front of the radiator. In fact, all of the cars were painted in some shade of gray, as was the Itala that won the Paris-Peking-Paris race in 1907.

The Züst, unlike some other competitors, had a New York State license, 19101 NY, attached to it for the start of the race. Unfortunately, the 1908 owner of this number is no longer recorded at the Department of Motor Vehicles for New York.

The race started on Feb. 12 in Times Square, and the Züst made it as far as Hudson on the first night, in company with the Thomas Flyer and the De Dion. Arthur Ruland, a sales manager of Züst in New York, was with the crew, as reported in Chicago. After many adventures and breakdowns later chronicled by Scarfoglio, including a large reception crowd and a day in the battered car for London via Folkestone at the behest of the *Daily Mail*, which had paid him for dispatches throughout the progress of the race. The car arrived in London with four men seated in it, but only Scarfoglio and possibly Haaga remained of the original crew. Scarfoglio visited the offices of the *Daily Mail*, the Züst concessionaire on Long Acre and the Franco-British Exhibition at the White City to display the car.

In a rash of bad luck, the car broke down on the way back to Folkestone and suffered a fire as gasoline was removed for rail transport at Bromley South rail station on Sept. 25. The mechanic doing the work, W. Maynard of Bromley, was badly burned and died from his injuries. Five days later, W.B. Sewell held a coroner's inquest in Bromley, the jury recording a verdict of death due to shock. Scarfoglio's subsequent comments reflected his attachment to the car: "The car is dead. It is irreparable." This probably caused the impression, which persists to this day, that the car was destroyed in a fire after the race was completed. Scarfoglio lost all of his notes and thus had to write his

book about the race from his diary and the dispatches he sent to the *Daily Mail* and other newspapers. Other local reports indicate that the local fire department was very prompt and saved the front portion of the car. The response to the alarm took just three minutes, and only the rear wheels and wooden body were severely damaged. The fire engine used has been preserved and can be viewed at the Kent Fire and Rescue Service in Maidstone.

The local reports also mention that some damaged parts, including the rear wheels, were taken back to the Züst showroom at Long Acre, near Covent Garden in London. The remainder of the car was looted by the local populace for souvenirs such as tanks, gasoline cans and charred papers. A photograph of the wreck, probably the one that later appeared in several publications, was taken by police constable George Charlo at 6:30 the following morning. The rear tires were completely burned, but the rims and spokes of the wheels were intact. The police's 1908 Occurrence Book, which would have recorded details of the incident, apparently has not survived.

The damaged and vandalized car was reportedly sent back to Milan with Scarfoglio, both leaving on the Folkestone ferry on Sept. 27, on the midday boat. The car was intended for a new body and wheels in time for the Paris salon. However, there is no mention of the car or the Züst Company in the program for the 1908 salon. The movements of the car from Folkestone are unknown. The French Line has no record of the car being shipped again to New York or anywhere else.

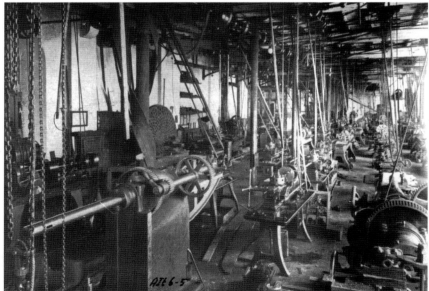

Years before the 1908 Great Race, Züst manufactured automobiles as early as 1905 at facilities in Milan, Italy, seen here. They were large and expensive models, with engines of 7.4 liters and 11.3 liters. In 1906, a separate company called Brixia-Züst was formed to produce smaller cars.

However, the presence of a New York State license plate on the car at the start of the race indicates ownership there, so the return of the car to the United States is reasonable. The car is now fitted with Healy detachable rims on the rear wheels, a modification that was only available in America in the early 1900s. The Healy Company, run by the same Raymond Healy who initiated Züst cars into competition in America, also did significant research into tires for arctic conditions just prior to the start of the Great Race. The appearance of the rims on the car is thus consistent with Raymond Healy's association with the Züst marque and the final destination of the car in Dawson City, Yukon. The rear

wheel spokes were "scorched" when the car arrived on Vancouver Island, suggesting that the original wheels taken to the Züst showroom at Long Acre in London may have been reunited with the chassis when it was returned to America.

The original route for the race included a foray across Alaska and the Yukon, including Dawson City, prior to crossing the Bering Sea on the winter ice. The organizers altered the route several times during the race, and the only car to make it to Alaska, the Thomas Flyer, was sent back to Seattle. Local anticipation of viewing the cars in Dawson City was dashed.

The 28/45 hp Tipo 1906 Züst with serial number 127 was obtained in New York by mining engineer O.B. Perry of the Yukon Gold Company and taken to Dawson City during or prior to mid-1910. In early August 1910, the Züst was "the only car in use" until Joe Boyle brought in a Flanders. Perry was the general manager and a director of Yukon Gold, which was run by the Guggenheims of New York. Robert Guggenheim was an automobile enthusiast in general and Italian automobiles in particular. He sponsored events such as a race from New York to Seattle in 1909, in which he entered an Itala.

The "Tipo 1906" is a reference to a design designation rather than the actual date of manufacture, as is common in many later Italian automobiles. An example is the Tipo 1750 Alfa Romeo, where the 1750 (cc) is the displacement of the engine. Another example is the racing Tipo 158 Alfetta, in which the "158" stood for 1.5 liters displacement and eight cylinders. The design notation is confirmed by a French article in late 1905 referring to the new 28/45 Züst as a "Modèle 1906." The chassis number 127 makes the likely date of chassis manufacture as late 1907, because the likely yearly production was about 50 to 60.

Perry visited the Yukon until at least 1915, but he only stayed a few days in the summer at that point. The "Guggenheim Automobile," driven by George

Potter, was still making news in Dawson in 1913, completing a winter road journey from Whitehorse to Dawson.

The ownership of the Züst from that time is undocumented, although it did stay in Dawson City. It was in Dawson until the 1950s, when Buck Rogers, an avid collector, bought it and took it to his residence in downtown Vancouver, B.C. The chassis was in two pieces by then and the car was inoperable. There it

stayed, untouched, evading an attempt to purchase it by William Harrah of Reno, who already had the race-winning Thomas Flyer. In 1980 it was sold and came to Vancouver Island, where it still resides in the ownership of Harry and Shirley Blackstaff, in restored condition.

The smaller Brixia-Züst line was powered by either the 1386cc three-cylinder or the 3770cc four-cylinder engine. Both had shaft drives.

Züst cars campaigned in later races in the United States. In March of 1909, V.P. Pisani, who was the general manager for Züst distributor R. Bertelli & Company in New York, obtained a perfect score in a New York to Boston endurance run. Pisani and Joseph Kingsland entered Züst automobiles in a hillclimb, for consistency with other stories in May 1910 at White

AUTHENTICATING THE GREAT RACE ZÜST

There are many reasons that No. 127 is the actual Great Race car, of which the following are the most important:

1. The frame, as noted by the *New York Times* in 1908, is stiffened and reinforced by the addition of top and bottom cover plates riveted to the frame channel sections from the front spring hangers to the cross member behind the flywheel. The gearbox also shows evidence of the altered gear ratios, accomplished by increasing the diameter, and thus the number of gear teeth, on the two drive-ring gears and the first and second gear wheels on the counter shaft. There are slots cut in the side and rear of the standard rectangular short wheelbase aluminum gearbox casting to accommodate each of these four larger gears.

The chassis is also modified by the addition of an extra transmission brake for a total of two. This was not normal on the short-chassis model, but was an available modification, due to its use on the intermediate-wheelbase car. The intermediate-wheelbase car also had a different shape for the gearbox casting, which has extensions at the first and second gear countershaft locations as well as extensions in the pinion locations. It is therefore possible that lower gear ratios from the larger car were substituted for the normal gears in the short-wheelbase chassis, accounting for the slots cut in the rectangular casing to accommodate the larger gears. These features are clearly shown on published chassis drawings for each wheelbase.

2. The front cylinders are unadorned cast iron, while the rear two have "Züst" cast into the top surface. The chassis drawing of the short-wheelbase car shows each cylinder with the "Züst" cast on top. The car suffered an oil-line failure on Feb. 10 in New York and had the front two cylinders replaced. The oil line is called a "broken tube of the injector" in the translated version of Scarfoglio's book and has been mistaken for the carburetor. The solder repair to the oil line is still on the car.

3. The car broke a driveshaft gear in Paxton, Neb., and had a new one shipped from New York via Omaha. The countershaft (driver side) ring gear in the car has neat, even, factory rivets fastening it to the driveshaft, while the mainshaft (passenger side) gear is obviously hand-riveted.

4. The car suffered an engine bearing failure near Kourga in Siberia at the end of June, and Haaga repaired the bearings by casting new ones from an alloy concocted from lead bullets and a tin lozenge box. The bearings from the rear two cylinders contain 97-percent lead and 3-percent tin (from a chemical analysis by an independent laboratory), while the front cylinder bearings are a normal high-tin Babbitt alloy.

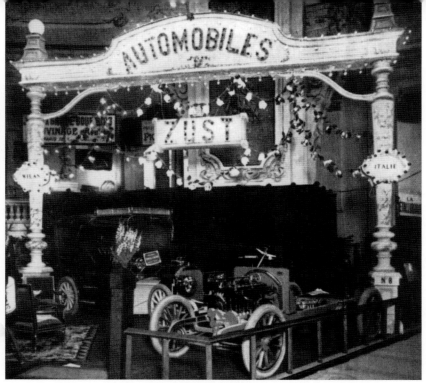

Above left: In the same year as the Great Race, another durable Züst was photographed at the Targa Bologna. Above right: At the 1906 Paris Auto Show. Below: Züst had a machine tool company and a foundry in Intra dating back to the turn of the century, when the company was just beginning to experiment with automobiles.

Plains, N.Y., in the class for the most-expensive cars (those over $4,000 and the only ones entered in the class). However, neither car actually competed in the climb. Jules Devigne competed with a Züst in a hill-climb won by Ralph de Palma in the summer of 1910.

In early 1910, the trophy for the New York to Paris race was awarded to the Thomas Flyer team in New York. It is over six feet high and weighs in excess of 1,600 pounds. The base is a combination of green Italian and pink French marble. There are medallions of German bronze depicting the coats of arms of the competing countries, and the trophy is topped by an American eagle. It is now in the National Automobile Museum in Reno, with the Thomas Flyer, as restored by William Harrah. The Protos was restored by the Siemens family and is in the Deutsches Museum in Munich. The restored Züst, as it is today, is shown in this article. We therefore have the unique situation in which all of the finishers of the longest automobile race ever sanctioned, more than 100 years ago, still exist in restored condition. AQ

Società Ing. ROBERTO ZÜST
Stabilimento di Intra Lago Maggiore.

THE MALMERSPACH BARN FIND

Arlette Schlumpf's Victory

There are few collections of vintage cars that have such a confusing history as the Malmerspach collection. Sixty-two unrestored cars, most of them as very rare and precious as the 17 Bugattis, had notable histories before their 45 years of seclusion. In fact, it was the reserve collection of Fritz Schlumpf. He bought 33 Bugattis from John Shakespeare, of fishing reel fame, in the United States in 1964 and brought them to Europe. Many of these will return to America this year to be displayed in Peter Mullin's new museum in Oxnard, Calif. In all those years, from then to now, nothing had been done to these cars, which had been sheltered by Schlumpf in a factory in Malmerspach, France.

BY ARNOUD AND ARD OP DE WEEGH

Hans Schlumpf was born in 1904 in Omegna, Italy, near Naples, his brother Fritz two years later. Their father died in 1918, so they were raised by their mother, Jeanne Schlumpf. This lady was quite strict and sparing; her sons both admired and feared her. In 1935, they started trading in wool and became textile industrialists in Mulhouse, France. By that time, Fritz had already taken part in a hillclimb with a Bugatti.

Jeanne Schlumpf died in 1957, and from that day on the brothers began collecting cars in a sort an exaggerated way. The Bugatti marque was a favorite, but not exclusively; they would often purchase a collection that included other historic or special-interest cars. In one of their factory halls in Malmerspach, they restored the cars with their own restoration team of as many as 10 specialists.

In 1977, a worldwide crisis in textile prices resulted from low production costs in Asia and forced the Schlumpf mills into bankruptcy. During a much-pub-

Above: The incomplete engine of the T40 (# 40902). Below: The Darmont Special.

licized revolt, the labor unions took possession of the properties, where they discovered 450 valuable cars, all expensively restored. They claimed that the money for this collection was stolen from the laborers. The Schlumpfs escaped to their Hotel des Trois Rois just up the road in Basel, Switzerland, and their property was confiscated. This was an unfair course of action, no doubt, because the bankruptcy was a result of the economic crisis in the textile industry. Fritz owed the factories money, but if he had sold one of the most expensive cars – the Bugatti Type 41 Royale, for example – he could have paid his debts. However, the French court didn't allow it, and the court also refused a financial guarantee from a Swiss bank. Fritz was sentenced *in absentia* to four years of prison after a tumultuous, intriguing and politically colored trial.

The fabulous car collection and its home were seized by the state and became one of the most important museums in the world, with 450 cars, including 112 Bugattis. The museum is situated in Mulhouse (*Automobile Quarterly* Vol. 37 No. 3). The unrestored reserve collection, stored in a barn in nearby

Malmerspach, was also taken from the Schlumpfs in 1977 and remained unprotected.

On April 18, 1992, Fritz Schlumpf died, disappointed, at the age of 86. In one respect, he was a victim of his love for cars. He certainly didn't get a fair trial. Fritz was not a saint, but he was willing to repair what he had done wrong; however, he didn't get the chance. He was sentenced without getting an opportunity for a real defense. There are rumors that his advisors were intimidated, and it seems fairly obvious that the press and the court had already sentenced him before his trial. After his death, his widow Arlette fought like a lioness to clear the name of her late husband. If the French government thought the fight was finished

Above and below: Many parts were stolen from a range of models.

after Fritz's death, they were mistaken. The rehabilitation of the Schlumpf name, for her late husband and their only daughter, became the most important thing in her life.

There were many judicial battles. Arlette wanted the museum to be called "The Schlumpf Museum," and she nearly succeeded; the official name is now "Cité de l'Automobile Musee National – Collection Schlumpf." For her, that was the first and most important rehabilitation of the Schlumpf name. Arlette wanted to show the world her husband did nothing wrong, and she wanted to expose the wrong attitude of the French court, the French government, the trade union, the laborers, the press and most of all, the bourgeoisie of Mulhouse. A lot has been written about the Schlumpf affair, but always from the point of view of the French authorities, the laborers and the trade union. And almost the whole world took their stand against the Schlumpfs. But there was another side to the story.

In 1999, the 62 cars of the Malmerspach Collection were returned to Arlette. For the French authorities, it was no more than a gesture, because the museum management believed that the amount of money needed for restoring the cars was more than the value of the cars. Besides, the cars were in much worse condition than they were in 1977. Access to the barn was quite easy, so lots of parts were stolen through the years. Almost all the steering wheels and Bugatti radiators were gone,

Above: Two Bugatti T57s. Below: The Bugatti engine with 3257cc capacity.

and the cars had been damaged as well. However, to Arlette, getting back a part of her late husband's car collection, even if it was only the unrestored reserve collection, was a victory.

She rented a barn in Wertolsheim, where she sheltered the Malmerspach Collection and refused to allow anyone to see the cars except for a few people she trusted. For many Bugatti enthusiasts, the Malmerspach Collection became an unreachable myth. The barn was drafty and damp, so the condition of the cars deteriorated.

In the meantime, Arlette wrote a book to tell her side of the story. The book was scheduled to be published in late 2008 or early 2009.

On May 16, 2008, Arlette died at the age of 76. Since 1977 she had been fighting, first in concert with her

Most cars survived in relatively good, restorable shape.

husband and then on her own, against the injustice that had been done to her family. In the author's opinion, she succeeded, although the museum cars were not returned to her. Because the French authorities appeared to give in to her demands, their behavior toward the Schlumpfs was not as "right" as it seemed to be.

Even during the last year of her life, Arlette negotiated with the later buyers of the collection to keep the most coveted parts together. And she succeeded. The buyers, Dutchman Jaap Braam Ruben and Frenchman Bruno Vendiesse, kept their word and sold the most beautiful part of the Malmerspach Collection to Peter Mullin in the United States. According to Mullin, he will only restore the Delage DB8 and the Peugeot Darl' Mat to "Pebble Beach condition." The other cars, including most of the Bugattis, will remain unrestored

and will be shown in his museum as a tribute to that brave French woman who fought almost half her life for the name of her husband.

About six weeks after Arlette's death, Jaap Braam Ruben and Bruno Vendiesse removed the cars from Wertolsheim. The less important part of the collection was moved to Prague and the other part, including Peter Mullin's cars, was moved to a small village near

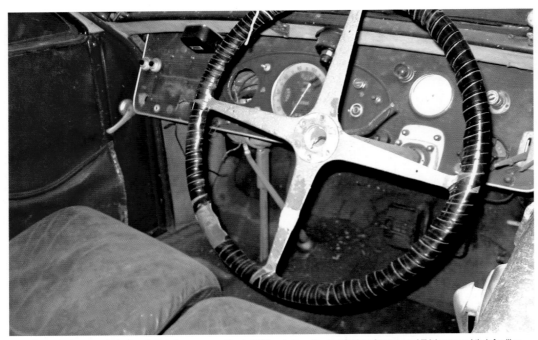

The collection had many exclusive brands, but also a common Peugeot 203 ambulance in which Schlumpf transported ill laborers and their families.

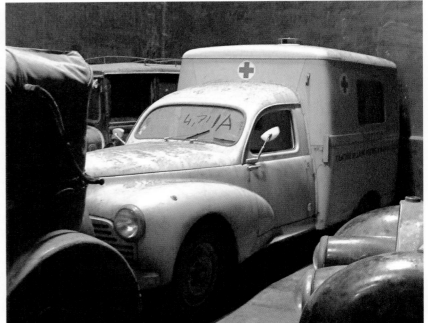

worth a fortune some decades later. In time, most of these cars would have ended up in a scrapyard. Yet he preserved them with his own money, and he was prepared to pay his debts. But, he was not allowed.

Walking between these cars, one cannot help but think of Arlette. The author never met her, but respect her he does. She never gave up. And her battle deserves to be continued. The cars will please many people in their unrestored beauty, as Mullin fully understands.

No, life doesn't end in death. Strong characters live on, and cars with character will stay beautiful in whatever condition.

Above: An already cleaned T40, an example of what a little water can do. Below: Among the several French finds is a Model T Ford.

Lille in France. Here, the cars waited to be shipped to the States.

On July 28, 2008, the author and his companions were allowed by Jaap and Bruno to come to France to photograph and film the collection before the major part would be shipped to America. Despite the theft of many parts, the first thing they saw was that most of the vehicles were in rather good condition and certainly restorable. Jaap and Bruno were busy buying replacements for these stolen items to make the cars complete. The visitors were struck by the mysticism of the cars. Certainly, the cars were a statement of "never giving up."

These cars radiated character and statement, perhaps more than the restored cars in the Schlumpf Museum – at least in their own right.

Before the author and his companions took their pictures, they walked amongst these historic cars, whispering. They halted by the Peugeot ambulance that Fritz Schlumpf bought to move his laborers or their families to a hospital in case of an emergency. Was this the man who was accused of stealing from his employees? We were impressed by the carefully chosen cars that Fritz intended to restore. Maybe pathetic, maybe overdone, but this man brought together an enormous collection. And he did this during a period when no one could know or expect that these vehicles would be

Size Does Matter

If you wait long enough, most goods come back into style. Today's Smart car, for example, is reminiscent of the microcars that turned up all over Europe in the mid-1940s, '50s and early '60s. Not far off from I-20 outside of Atlanta, Bruce Weiner has put together the largest single collection of microcars in the world. With more than 300 cars, his Microcar Museum, which opened in 1997, is a one-of-a-kind preservation of automobile history of the post-World War II era.

BY PETER HILDEBRANDT

After the devastation of the war, many were unable to afford a car. Newly out-of-work German aircraft makers like Messerschmitt and Heinkel, among others, put their efforts into designing and manufacturing small, affordable cars that would get people out of the elements and into an auto. Thus, the microcar was reborn. (After WWI, there were the "forecars" and cyclecars prior to the 1930s.) However, this time around, microcars were the product of a great deal of new engineering talent. For the first time, that generation was able to afford a convenient personal transport that also had a bright new image and style.

Besides its low price and great gas mileage, most had three wheels, which made it possible to avoid a road tax in Europe. And with engines under 50 cc, a driver's license was not required.

Over a period of 10 years, Goggomobil built some 280,000 autos, which put it at the top for popularity, most likely because the Goggomobil had the most features of a full-size car, like radio and heater. It could also seat four.

DRIVING INSIDE A BUBBLE

Though microcars were noisy, often crude and not very reliable, they provided transport for thousands of motorists, which gave them a crucial role in motoring history. Because of their shape, many of these vehicles were nicknamed "bubblecars." In a sweet kind of irony, the company Weiner's family owned is well known to kids of all ages as Double Bubble. The chewing gum giant is now in Canada after being bought out by Tootsie Roll. But Weiner named the land on which the museum is located "Double Bubble Acres."

The thing that immediately dazzles visitors to Weiner's museum is color. Aside from the 300-plus vibrantly painted vehicles filling the floor, walls are loaded with microcars and other 20th century memorabilia, and a good share of neon signs, vintage vending machines and coin-operated children's rides.

Ninety percent of the cars on the floor run. The biggest make of microcar represented is the Messerschmitt, and there are also quite a few Isettas and Goggomobils.

The optimal speed of most microcars is approximately 45 mph, according to Jim Janecek, editor of *The Vintage Microcar Club – Microcar News* (www.microcar.org). Janecek points out the history of microcars dating back

all the way to post-World War I times. At first, their development came about as a way to deal with the profusion of disabled war veterans at that time in Europe.

"French pedal cars eventually had a pair of pedals so that even a blinded husband – who could still help out by pedaling while his wife steered – would maintain some sense of self-worth, as well as help with mobility," Janecek said. The Microcar Museum has a few of these types of cars. The 1935 Velocar Camionette started life as a pedals-only car, but was fitted with a noisy, primitive aftermarket motor, common for the times.

The Messerschmitt also had its beginnings as an invalid car for war veterans from World War II who had lost limbs. "It wasn't actually manufactured for that purpose, but the individual originally designing it initially intended for these vehicles to help veterans be able to get around," Janecek said.

Fritz Fend designed and built what became known as the Fend Flitzer. "Initially it was propelled by a kind of rowing action and later evolved into a motor vehicle with a tiny 35cc engine," says Adam Quellin, author of *Microcars at Large!* "Further changes were made, including stronger wheels and tires. Eventually, after more changes, the vehicle became known as the Kabinenroller (meaning cabin scooter). Fend needed a bigger factory in which to work and so enlisted the help of his former boss – Messerschmitt. Messerschmitt provided the financial backing and the use of his former aircraft factory, and his name was given to the car. Despite appearances, Messerschmitts were not made from surplus aircraft parts."

Turns out, most of the people purchasing the cars were not invalids; they were actually purchased by people as cheap transportation, according to Janecek. "A regular car then cost a lot of money, and many people couldn't afford them. Marketing emphasized they were not much more than scooters, something people were quite familiar with.

Opposite: Perhaps the epitome of personal transport, a 2001 Corbin Sparrow. Above: Among dozens of other microcars in Bruce Weiner's collection is the 1956 Avolette Tourisme (left).

Only now they could get out of the rain too, while scooting around."

According to Quellin, full-sized second-hand cars fetched ridiculous prices. Waiting lists for new cars, for those who could afford them, were often years long. The microcar changed that. After WWII, manufacturers produced: 280,000 Goggomobils; more than 50,000 Messerschmitt Kabinenrollers; 24,484 Bond Minicars (all types); 161,728 BMW Isettas; 7,115 Velam Isettas; 6,000 Iso Isettas; 3,090 Romi Isettas; and many other makes too numerous to mention.

A TINY CAR

The definition of a microcar can get a bit complicated, but few will disagree that it is an extremely small automobile. The Bruce Weiner Microcar Museum describes them as: "Engine sizes of 700 cc and less and two doors or less."

Depending on whom who you're talking to, the dimensions might include "less than three meters in length" and "less than 85 cubic feet (2400 liters) interior volume." Most definitions also involve multiple parameters, and of those, engine size – or lack of – is is very important.

The Weiner collection includes a 1966 Peel Trident. This microcar, and the 1962 Peel P-50, the smallest car ever, were manufactured on the Isle of Man in England. Approximately 47 cars were built from October 1963 to December 1964. The sign next to the car describes it as a tiny 4-ft. 2-in.-long car mounted to a chair on go-kart wheels surrounded by a close-fitting angular fiberglass body. *"Powered (using the term loosely) by a 49 cc Zweirad Union (DKW) moped motor underneath the driver, it generated more noise than power. At an advertised 100 miles per gallon, it was "almost cheaper than walking." A contemporary road test joked that the top speed was dependent upon the size of the steak that the driver had for dinner."*

At the Microcar Museum there are two electrics, a BMW Hazel and the Manocar. Shelves at the far end hold cars waiting to be restored. A bright neon green car, is a rare Italian Julian from 1947. Another one, its sister car is on the rack above it, awaiting restoration.

You can take a virtual tour of the museum online at www.microcarmuseum.com.

The museum isn't open every day, so visitors might want to call before taking a trip there.

Every two years, on Memorial Day weekend, a Microcar Meet is held on the premises. The next event will be in May 2009. Participants travel from all around the country, and the world, to take part in the event. Some may bring their cars, others don't, and you don't have to have a microcar to show up, although you do have to preregister.

There's a special interest group at every MIcrocar Meet. At the last meeting, the group was Cushman Scooters and King Midget. The previous meet featured Triumph, and before that was the Vespa Club.

OUT OF THE BARN AND INTO THE LIGHT

Each car at the museum has a story. Twenty-one of Weiner's microcars had once been parked in The Automuseum Warstein-Belecke Germany, which was owned by a Mr. Berger, who opened the museum in 1976. After his death three years later, his widow closed up the barn, and the cars gathered dust.

Weiner tracked down the collection. In October and November 2004, he was able to purchase them, and the

came to regret his decision. He then went about re-acquiring microcars, including some of those he'd sold from his first collection.

MICROCARS IN AMERICA

Among the microcars, the vast majority of which are from Europe, there were a few American brands, ones most of us have probably never heard of. The American Eshelman was sold in kit form through ads in the back of *Popular Science*

In a copy of the August 1955 *Mechanix Illustrated*, an ad for the kit microcar tells readers that for $25 dollars they can "build a Pony Roadster or Pick-up in a few spare hours. Uses 2 hp engine, can pick up 450 lb. loads, gets 70 mpg and very low-cost assembly from parts bought in your neighborhood. Uses home tools, great for kids and a sturdy utility car. Complete step-by-step plans with 15 large-size pages and 24 'show-how' photos."

Other microcars appear in the same issue, including a Special King Midget Sports car offered as second prize in the magazine's "Buildwords Contest." The

From the interesting to the bizarre (from left): a 1959 Bond Minicar MK F, a pedal-powered 1938 Velocar Type H, and a 1965 Hillers.

microcars were shipped to Madison, Ga. Some simply needed a good bath, but others needed new tires and a bit more care to make it onto the display floor. A few are still in storage awaiting future restoration.

These days, microcars can be found at times for sale on e-bay or they are obtained, as is often the case for Weiner, through word of mouth. He has friends living in Europe who will let him know when they find out about a car.

Weiner's first collection was based in Ontario, Canada. He sold the whole collection at an auction at Christie's. A framed picture of those first microcars hangs on the wall behind the museum's information desk. Some time after the sale of the cars, Weiner

and *Popular Mechanics*. A large poster near the entrance for the Eshelman features the famous 1950s actor Bob Cummings promoting the cars, showing his three children riding in a pair of Eshelmans. A blurb in the corner of the poster invites us to "See Bob Cummings on TV."

The King Midget, developed by Claud Dry and Dale Orcutt, who met during WWII when they were both Civil Air Patrol pilots, was manufactured in Athens, Ohio, starting out as a kit car, though later it could be also be purchased fully assembled. According to the International King Midget Car Club, Inc, the King Midget was the only small car continuously manufactured for nearly a quarter of a century.

King Midget was valued at $569 dollars. (First prize in the contest was a new Ford Thunderbird, valued at more than $3,000.) Sixth prize was an American-made Eshelman Sports Car, "with a 3-hp air-cooled engine, automatic clutch and starter. Ideal for short trips to work, the beach or to shop. Speeds to 25 mph, 70 mpg; one adult or two children, valued at $395."

Further on in that same issue is a full-page photo layout and description of a "Thunderbird Jr." This is billed as a "sidewalk-sized" replica version of the full-sized T-bird. When the child takes the foot off the accelerator, the vehicle automatically stops. As the write-up sums it up, "The price, Pop, is about $400." This looks to be the extent to which Americans

from those limited attempts to interest the public in the microcar phenomenon, the idea never took off. Perhaps because the postwar years in this country didn't leave us with a ravaged country – we were one of the few in the world to come out of the war with our infrastructure virtually unscathed – we didn't feel the need to think small, efficient and inexpensive. Likely, with the Great Depression finally over, Americans preferred to have their vehicles big and fast, as witnessed by the models sold in the decades after WWII.

THE END OF THE ROAD, OR JUST THE START?

Prosperity, among other things, eventually did in the microcar at the early part of the 1960s. New small cars were appearing that were not much more expensive than microcars. More materials became available for larger auto manufacture. The introduction of the Mini was another factor in the death of the microcar. It was introduced in 1959, according to Quellin.

involved themselves in microcars, mainly as novelty items, toys for children or contest prizes.

Some time ago, one of the museum's regular visitors brought in an old article from the 1950s describing how a Buick dealership in Arizona offered an Isetta microcar with the purchase of a new car off the lot. German-made Messerschmitts may have been offered at Cadillac dealerships with a purchase of their cars as well.

Microcars in the United States never really caught on. The cars were manufactured on a large scale in 14 other countries, however, including Germany, Spain, the United Kingdom, Italy and Brazil. Modifications were done to the models sold in America, but aside

Toy-like as they are, microcars can be considered a microcosm of "fun on wheels." Top left: 1961 Taylor Dunn Trident. Above: Eschelman child sports cars.

"It could carry four people, had a more reliable, more powerful engine but with tiny proportions," Quellin said. "Some microcars evolved over time and became more refined and 'car like' as people's expectations grew. The Fiat 500 survived and continued to be produced until the 1970s. The Citroen 2CV was

today. "The French company Aixam produces a 500cc small car, as does Ligier. Another company, actually called Microcar, produces a small hatchback along similar lines. These cars are usually fitted with a 505cc Lombardini diesel engine and CVT (Constantly Variable Transmission) belt drive. Piaggio still makes

the Ape (pronounced 'Ah-pay,' meaning 'wasp'), small three-wheeled vans and pickup trucks. They range from 50cc-capacity engines up to around 400 cc. There is the successful smart car, which is now being exported to the States."

Quellin believes the demand for microcars will increase: "However, the priority will shift from one of economy to environmental issues, space saving and visual appeal. Modern motorists want a trendy 'green' image. Another factor that is often overlooked is that of embedded environmental impact. This is the resources and energy used to manufacture the car in the first place. The ideal microcar would need to be 'low impact' in every sense."

As they say, history repeats itself. Or maybe it's just the same thing over and over. But when it comes to microcars, a visitor can't help but think while walking away from all those shining, sleek – and tiny – cars: "I sure could use one of them right now." AQ

Above left: 1961 Fiat Giardiniera. Above right: Inside a Messerschmitt. Below: The attractive IHLE Schottenring Car.

made right up until 1990. The Volkswagen Beetle was not much more expensive than many microcars and was often the preferred choice."

Quellin has always been fascinated with old cars. "Microcars have the additional benefits of being lightweight, small and economical with loads of character. They attract more attention than larger, more exotic vehicles. They may be slower, but offer more 'smiles per gallon.'"

Bruce Weiner seems to feel the same way. When he saw a Messerchmitt for the first time in 1991, he bought one right away. After that, it just became a disease, he said. "The fun factor with these little cars is enormous." Weiner's dedication to preserving this part of automotive history is evident in his impeccable preservation of each car.

When asked about the future of the microcar, Quellin says that microcars are very much with us

Going Micro

The Trucks of Mario Palma

Mario Palma has been a keen car and truck enthusiast all his life. He has an undying passion for microcars and trucks, but anything on wheels can turn up in the Palma Automobile Collection, including – and most interestingly – microtrucks.

BY NORM MORT
PHOTOGRAPHY BY ANDREW MORT

As a teenager, Mario drove many of the big trucks, pickups and even dozers while working at his father's construction company. It was at that time he developed a particular fondness for Mack trucks. Yet, Mario's first collector vehicle was a stock 1949 Chevy Deluxe Coupe he purchased in 1986. Engine problems resulted in its quick sale, in favor of a 1932 Ford Model B Stake truck. Trucks were more to his interest, so it wasn't long before an even larger and rarer flatbed 1939 Mack EGX was purchased and restored. Others soon followed.

Over the next few years, Mario filled what most of us would consider a very large garage. In the mid-1990s, he decided to sell all his big trucks, except for the Ford Model B, as he had discovered the world of microcars and microtrucks.

His first microcar purchase was a 1957 BMW 300 that he bought from a collector. "I've driven this one the most, but then I've had it the longest. It's a favorite of most people."

Mario's love of trucks soon had him seeking the commercial versions of microcars. Two of the rarest are his personal favorites: the IsoCarro trucks based on the ISO Isetta design. "I still wanted trucks and these were micros. Interestingly, I had a picture of an IsoCarro pickup for a business card years before."

Other trucks, vans and wagons from Fiat and Autobianchi were added, but his fascination with micros was not limited to national borders. "I found the French microcars the most interesting, but I own more Italian examples. It's not because I'm Italian, but rather because of a good contact in Italy."

German, French, Japanese and English micros were all part of the quickly growing collection. One of his oldest microcars is a beautifully restored 1937 Fiat Topolino. "I really like the old micros, but these vehicles are much harder to find."

Honda started small, in both its organization and its products. Here, Honda's 1984 Zoe Zipper, powered by a 49cc engine. Only a dozen were U.S. imports.

Containers filled with microcars, as well as scooters, arrived from Europe at his offices north of Toronto, Ontario, on a regular basis over the next five years. Many of the most uncommon models required extensive restorations, but where possible, he purchased clean, original or restored examples. The collection grew quickly, and although a self-placed limit was set at 40, that number grew to 50 and eventually 60.

By 2000, it was clear that the extended garage at home, his office and an industrial unit were no longer large enough.

Mario's dream had always been to house his collection in one building for permanent display. He acquired a farm north of Toronto and built a large compound that included a two-story building with an elevator, a storage and workshop facility for parts and maintenance, and an area for displaying some of his collection outside. Here his microvehicles were put on exhibit along with scooters, antique tricycles, some military and fire trucks, tractors, pedal cars, household antiques and a vintage power tool collection.

RAREST OF THE RARE

Of the many rare vehicles in the Palma Collection, the most unusual are the IsoCarro trucks. While other collectors may have Spanish-built versions, the Palma Collection has five Italian-built IsoCarros.

By the early 1950s, ISO had established itself as a builder of motor scooters, motorcycles, and other vehicles, and it was ISO that designed the tiny egg-shaped Isetta. Variations of the original Isetta would be built in Germany, Belgium, Britain, France, Spain and Brazil.

Introduced in 1953 at the Turin Auto Show, the ISO was an immediate sensation, yet from 1953 to 1955 ISO delivered just 4,900 units. In comparison, BMW, under license, built 161,728 Isettas by the time production was halted in May 1962.

Still, at the time of introduction, ISO had great plans for its Isetta, designed by aeronautical genius

Ermenegildo Preti. The company saw a commercial possibility in offering small ISO trucks, using the Isetta as a basis. The body was extensively modified and mounted on an extended tubular chassis to support a platform, pickup box or cube van body. Brochures depicted an Isetta als Kipper (dump truck), als Feuerwehr (ladder truck), AutoCarro (platform truck) and a carrier. Most enthusiasts believed these were only concepts until the trucks were discovered and restored as part of the Palma Collection.

Also in the collection are five German-built Isettas in various guises, a French Velam and a Brazilian 1958 Romi awaiting restoration.

Other Italian delights in the collection include six Autobianchi and Fiat vans. Bianchi built just 50 cars a day at its Desio (Milan, Italy) plant, compared to the Fiat 500's 300 per day. The Autobianchi models, of the popular Fiat 500, were stylish, up-market versions popular with small businesses such as florists and bakeries. The Bianchina vans featured additional chrome and more luxurious interiors and trim, as well as additional sound insulation and a slightly more powerful engine that was laid flat to increase cargo capacity.

The collection's four-cylinder 1948 Fiat Topolino 500B Furgone and 1950 Fiat Topolino 500C Cassone are special examples of the popular Topolino models that reached 519,646 units by the time production ended in 1954.

The early Topolino vans and pickups were used mainly by the Italian army prior to 1945, and none are known to exist. It's rumored that there are as many as 10 of the, perhaps, 50 500B vans still surviving, but few are ever seen outside Italy. The one in the collection had, at one point, been driven by an iron worker who used the Furgone as a daily driver.

There are no records of how many of the Fiat 500C Topolino van and pickup versions were built. A few exist today, but some pickup trucks have since been fabricated out of sedans.

Mario's vans are totally original, other than having been recently painted for photographic reasons. Both are slated for future concours restorations, but presently

Preceding page and above: The resemblance to aircraft – albeit, small aircraft – was the Inter, powered by a 175cc Ydral 8.5hp single-cylinder engine.

a handsome 1939 NSU-Fiat 500 Weinsberg roadster is undergoing a complete rebuild.

In addition to these Italian models, the Palma Collection features Fiat and Bianchina Giardinera models, two 1960 Fiat Jollys – a 500 and a 600 are currently being restored – as well as a popular 1959 Fiat 600 Multipla.

A seldom-seen Italian version of the Messerschmitt is a 1956 Mi-Val Milvalino. Mi-Val built motorcycles and three-wheelers in Italy from 1950 to 1960 and fitted its own 171.7cc engine. And, of course, no microvehicle collection is complete without a Piaggio Ape.

As well as the Isettas, German micros include a Goggomobil Dart (a German transplant that was actually built in Australia), a Janus Zundapp and a mini-van-like 1958 Lloyd LT600.

MICRO USE AROUND THE WORLD

Europe and North America have very few micro-cars and trucks currently in production, whereas Japan, India and other parts of Asia have large markets for these tiny vehicles and have always offered a wide array. In Japan, microvehicles became popular transportation in the 1950s. Daihatsu may not be a familiar make in North America, but it's one of the largest producers of microvehicles in Japan today. In the collection is a 1959 Daihatsu Trimobile pickup that was used for years as a fish truck on the U.S. west coast. It features a vinyl, snap-on sunroof, suicide doors, and a 12hp, 305cc single-cylinder, two-stroke engine with a three-speed manual transmission.

Mazda is a far more familiar nameplate, and its early entries into the vehicle market included numerous three-wheel trucks, but its first car was the tiny R360 coupe that appeared in 1960, powered by an air-cooled V2 engine. Capable of a top speed of 56 mph, the 1962 version in the collection had a different rear window fitted in the past.

A more modern Japanese vehicle is a 1984 Honda Zoe Zipper, powered by a 49cc engine. It was one of just a dozen imported into the United States by Honda to be used at its assembly facilities for executives. Originally in coupe form, the tops were removed for plant tours.

From France, there are numerous examples of New Map models. Founded in 1920 by Paul Martin, New Map first focused on motorcycles and scooters. In 1938, the company introduced its first car, manufactured by a sister company, under the Rolux name.

By 1949, this New Map division was known as Societe Rolux in Clermont-Ferrand and offered the Rolux Baby VB 61, powered by a 6hp, 175cc, two-stroke air-cooled engine. An estimated total of 1,000 Rolux cars were built from 1938 until 1952, when production ceased in favor of its more popular scooters and a range of three-wheeled goods-carrying vehicles. Production increased over the next four years.

The New Map, three-wheel, Solyto microtrucks were built by the company's sheet-metal division, known as the Societe Lyonnaise de Tolerie. These unusual French trucks were offered in different body styles to suit the needs of both farmers and business people. The Solyto's dated styling even, in 1956, didn't hurt demand as production continued until 1974. Over the years, power plants ranged from a two-stroke, 125cc Ydral, air-cooled engine mounted on the front wheel to a similar-sized Ultima engine offered with an automatic transmission, and in New Map's final years, a KV unit. It's estimated that 4,000 Solyto microtrucks were built during 18 years of production.

Microcars are often referred to as being egg-shaped, and that term certainly applies to the two-stroke,

125cc, single-cylinder fiberglass, chain-drive 1956 Paul Vallee Chantecler with its rubber suspension. Production was very limited over a five-year period, and even fewer survive of this unusual three-wheeler.

The French also built an aircraft-like micro in the form of the SNCAN Inter, powered by a 175cc Ydral 8.5hp, two-stroke, single-cylinder engine mounted in the rear. The Inter had innovative, fold-up front wheels for parking in the narrowest of spots, but this feature

was later abandoned due to cost and complications.

Microcars are generally considered more of a 1950s and 1960s phenomenon, but micros continued to be offered in various markets to the present day. One of the smallest microcars ever built was the French-built Mini Comtesse, unveiled in the mid-1970s. The collection's 1975 fully enclosed model is powered by a 50cc engine with an automatic transmission.

Another '70s micro was the 1975 William. Its boxy

The Italian version of the micro Messerschmitt is this 1956 Mi-Val Milvalino. Mi-Val produced motorcycles and three-wheeled vehicles in Italy from 1950-1960.

design would certainly fit into the current styling wave. Its success was hampered by its woefully underpowered, 125cc, two-stroke engine that provided a top speed of just over 40 mph.

The British were also fond of microcars, with Bond and Reliant being the best known. Mario Palma chose other British models for his collection. An open four-wheel, twin-cylinder, Villiers-powered Frisky Sport was converted to three-wheel guise, while a second is under restoration. The British Frisky was advertised in 1958 just before the Earl's Court unveiling as "Britain's answer to world demand" and "The Car People Have Been Waiting For!" It was manufactured by Henry Meadows of prewar engine fame, and the entire project was originally conceived and designed by racing driver Captain Raymond Flower and his brothers. That initial design was rejected in favor of a design created by former Kieft personnel Gordon Bedson, who had

originally joined Meadows as export sales manager, and Keith Peckmore, who crafted the prototype chassis. Further refinement resulted in a very stylish gullwing-coupe design, by Italian Michelotti, which was built by Vignale of Turin for the Geneva Auto Show in 1957. Due to anticipated production costs, over the ensuing 18 months the Frisky was completely restyled again and appeared in open Sport form with rear hinged doors.

The Frisky shares space with a British 1963 Heinkel-based Trojan, a 1959 Opperman Unicar, a 1960 Scootacar and a 1959 Nobel 200.

With space already at a premium, an extension to Mario's collection is being planned to house the recent arrival of such vintage giants of the road as a Studebaker COE, an Autocar, various Mack trucks of the 1940s and 1950s, a 1955 Tatra 805 military truck, a 1944 Chevrolet COE fire truck and more.

The Palma Collection is currently not open to the public, but special group tours may be arranged. ◄○►

Above: One of the smallest of the small, the French-built Mini Comtesse was unveiled in the mid-1970s. This 1975 model requires a 50cc engine for propulsion.
Opposite page: 1959 Fiat 600 Multipla van.

NOTES AND COMMENTARY

CONTACTING AQ

Automobile Quarterly, ISSN 0005-1438, ISBN ISBN 1-59613-060-1 (978-1-59613-060-9), is published quarterly by Automobile Heritage Publishing and Communications, LLC. Editorial and publication offices: 800 East 8th Street, New Albany, Indiana, USA 47150. Telephone (812) 948-AUTO (2886); fax (812) 948-2816; e-mail info@autoquarterly.com; Web site www. autoquarterly.com.

SUBSCRIPTION SERVICE

For subscriptions, back issues, indexes, reader service, changes of address, and order entry, call (866) 838-2886. If calling from Indiana or outside the U.S., call (812) 948-2886. Back issue prices start at $25.95, plus shipping. For domestic subscription orders: 1 year (4 issues), $79.95; 2 years (8 issues), $149.95; 3 years (12 issues), $199.95. For Canadian orders: 1 year, $99.95; 2 years, $189.95; 3 years, $259.95. For all other international orders: 1 year, $109.95; 2 years, $209.95; 3 years, $289.95. Mastercard, Visa, or American Express are accepted. Order online at www.autoquarterly.com. To order by mail, please send check or money order to *AQ/Automobile Quarterly*, 1950 Classic Car Circle, P.O. Box 1950, New Albany, IN 47151. The fax number for orders is (812) 948-2816.

POSTMASTER

Please send all changes of address to: *Automobile Quarterly*, P.O. Box 1950, New Albany, IN 47151. Periodical postage paid at New Albany, Indiana, and at additional mailing offices.

OPPORTUNITY

Details of fund raising programs for car clubs and automobile museums are available by calling (812) 948-AUTO (2886).

Cover & Contents
Art by Bernie Fuchs.

Camoradi Maserati Birdcage
Black-and-white photography: p. 4 courtesy Carl Moore; p. 6, 7 (bottom) courtesy Simon Lewis Transport; p. 7 (top) from Pete Lyons; p. 8 courtesy Dave Friedman; p. 9, 10, 11, 12 (top) from Walter Baumer; p. 12 (bottom) courtesy Tom Farrington; p. 13 courtesy Indianapolis Motor Speedway.
Color Photography: pp. 4-5, 13 courtesy Carl Moore; p. 10 courtesy Leigh Dorrington; p. 14 courtesy Vanderbilt Concours d'Elegance; p. 15 courtesy Kyle Burt.

Bibliography
Barnett, Randy. "Lords of the Ring," *Automobile Quarterly*, Vol. 47, No. 1, 2007;
Baeumer, Walter. Deutcher Maserati Club, correspondence, 2008;
Finn, Joel. *Maserati Birdcage*, Osprey Publishing Limited, 1980;
Gurney, Dan. Personal interview, December 2007;
Haler, Justin, "The Story of the Birdcage Maserati," *Autosport*, December 1970;
Ibing, Hartmut. Correspondence, 2008;
Ludvigsen, Karl. *Dan Gurney*, Haynes Publishing, 2000;
Menard, Pierre and Vassal, Jacques. *Stirling Moss, The Champion Without a Crown*, Chronosports S.A., 2003;
Moss, Sir Stirling. Personal interview, 2008;
Oosthoek, Willem. *Birdcage to Supercage*, Dalton Watson Fine Books Limited, 2004;
Prichard, Anthony. *Maserati, A Racing History*, Haynes Publishing, 2003;
Wagner, Carl L. "Maserati," *Automobile Quarterly*, Vol. 5 No. 3, 1967;
Wimpffen, Janos. *Time and Two Seats*, Motorsport Research Group, 1999.

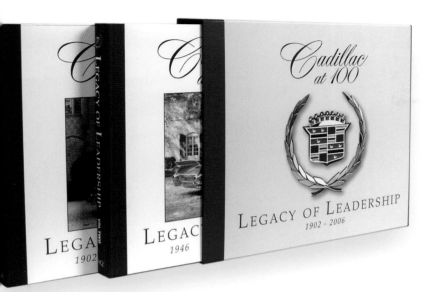

Cadillac at 100: Legacy of Leadership

Cadillac at 100: Legacy of Leadership

Vol. 1 ISBN: 978-1-59613-001-2
Vol. 2 ISBN: 978-1-59613-002-9
Two-volume set, with slipcase
560 pages
230+ color photographs

$99.95 + $19.00 s&h UPS

Cadillac at 100: Legacy of Leadership is an authoritative, intimately fascinating story with which no Cadillac enthusiast can do without. More than 230 full-color photographs of Cadillacs through model-year 2008, with every model, every event, and every period painstakingly covered, promise much for the Cadillac lover.

This updated edition of the previously titled *Cadillac: Standard of the World* provides an unprecedented look at the company that has truly set the standard in terms of luxury, performance and craftsmanship. Read about how founder Henry Leland, with his obsession over precision, planned the course for the manufacturer that has not only survived volatile market conditions and changing consumer demand, but also has thrived in its position as the standard bearer for GM.

Inside this 560-page, two-volume set, readers will discover the people and the programs that continue to make Cadillac a name associated with success. Intimate interviews with the major players – from the days of Henry Leland and the Thirty to the days of Mark LaNeve and the Escalade – accompany a litany of technological milestones and model descriptions. *Cadillac at 100: Legacy of Leadership* is destined to become the bible for both researchers and casual enthusiasts, a cornerstone for any collector's library.

VOLUME 48 NO.4

The Wayne Automobile

Author West Peterson is editor of the Antique Automobile Club of America's magazine *Antique Automobile*. Photos by the author.

Contact Information

Antique Automobile Club of America
501 W. Governor Rd.
P.O. Box 417
Hershey, PA 17033
Phone (717) 534-1910
Fax: (717) 534-9101
www.aaca.org

The Patterson Collection

A huge debt of gratitude is owed The Patterson Collection from all the classic car fans for restoring, maintaining and sharing these remarkable art pieces. And a special "thanks" is extended to Jim I, Jim II, Tom and Brennan for their efforts and southern hospitality that made this article possible.

All photos courtesy of the author.

Stuttgart Calling

This feature article is excerpted and adapted from a chapter in the recently released volume titled *Ferdinand Porsche: Genesis of Genius*. The book is authored by marque expert Karl Ludvigsen and

published by Bentley Publishers (see this issue's "AQ Book Review" for more information). Special thanks to Maurice Iglesias at Bentley Publishers for assisting with this project.

Black-and-white photos: pp. 34, 36, 37, 38, 40, 43 courtesy Bentley Publishers; pp. 39, 40, 42 from the AQ Photo and Research Archive.

Contact Information

Club Information
Porsche Club of America
P.O. Box 1347
Springfield, VA 22151-0347

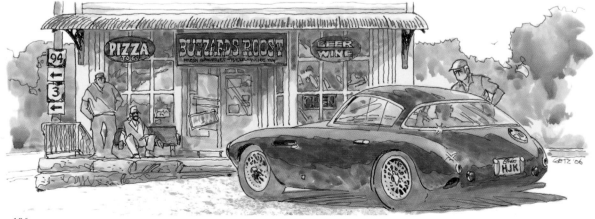

Phone: (703) 321-2111
Fax: (703) 321-2110
www.pca.org

Art Gallery with Bernie Fuchs

The author is grateful to Bernie Fuchs for the opportunity to share the story of his extraordinary career; to Bernie and Babe Fuchs for entrusting me with invaluable original art to illustrate the story; and to *AQ* managing editor Tracy Powell for sharing the opportunity. The author also wishes to acknowledge the significant contributions of Davis Apatoff in *Illustration* and Linda Price in *American Artist*.

Bibliography

Apatoff, David. "The Art of Bernie Fuchs," *Illustration*, Issue 15, 2005;
Price, Linda S. "Fine Art or Illustration," *American Artist*, December 2008;
Fuchs, Bernie. Personal interviews, 2008.

Col. Green's Hybrid Cars

Special thanks to Mark Lizewskie, curator of the Jack W. Rich Collection, and Barbara Bedell Fortin for their assistance in editing as well as providing historical photographs and information included in this article.

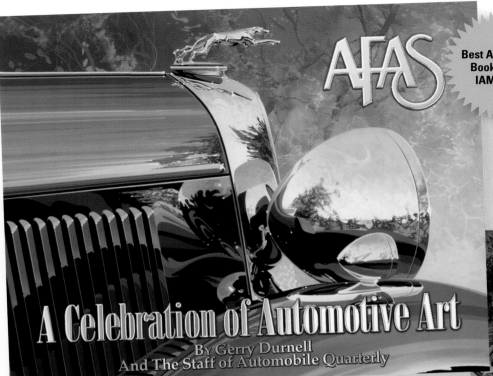

Come meet the world's top echelon of automotive artists in *Automobile Quarterly*'s book, *A Celebration of Automotive Art*, a masterful compendium of the fine art and artists of the Automotive Fine Art Society (AFAS). Articles capturing the unique personalities of all 32 artists of the AFAS are complemented by striking reproductions of their work, including the latest paintings and sculptures.

Step into the world of artistic elegance and top-shelf talent, where behind-the-canvas interviews reveal artists' impressions and philosophies. See for yourself what makes these masters tick, what stirs the passion that translates into powerful expression. This ultimate coffee-table book also covers the work and biographies of deceased luminaries such as Peter Helck, Walter Gotschke and Carlo Demand.

Lincoln Motor Car Co. announced the book's release at the 2005 Pebble Beach Concours d'Elegance, marking the 10-year anniversary of Lincoln sponsorship of AFAS at the event, and the Society's 20th Anniversary. Order your copy of *A Celebration of Automotive Art* today.

AFAS:
A Celebration of Automotive Art

ISBN 978-1-59613-005-0
374 pages, 14 x 11 (horizontal)
Hardbound with dustjacket and slipcase

$125

Order Today: Toll-free Phone (866) 838-2886 • Fax (812) 948-2816 • Outside the U.S., Call Direct (812) 948-2886

Black-and-white photography courtesy of the collections of John W. Rich and Barbara Fortin.
Color photography by Denis Tanney.

Bibliography
Author Unknown. "Rauch & Lang/Stearns-Knight Gasoline Electric Automobile," *The Knight-Overland Starter*, First Quarter 1990, No. 111;

Bedell, Barbara Fortin. *Colonel Edward Howland Robinson Green and the World He Created at Round Hill,* South Dartmouth, Mass., 2003;

Duerksen, Menno. "Free Wheeling," *Cars & Parts*, December 1968;

Kimes, Beverly Rae and Clark Jr., Henry Austin. *Standard Catalog of American Cars 1805-1942, Third Edition*, Krause Publications, Iola,Wis., 1996;

Marvin, Keith. "The Colonel's Curious Conveyances," *Special Interest Autos* #108, December 1988;

Ruddock, Ken. "Recharging an Old Idea, The Hundred-Year History of Electric Cars," *Automobile Quarterly*, Vol. 31, No. 1, 1992, Kutztown Publishing Co., Kutztown, Pa.;

Wells, Stuart W. "Car of a Thousand Speeds, The Entz System and Owen Magnetic," Automobile Quarterly, Vol. 36, No. 3, 1997, Kutztown Publishing Co., Kutztown, Pa.;

Zahm, Karl S. "The Classic Rauch & Lang, An Electrifying Motorcar," *The Classic Car*, Volume XXXVIII, No. 3, September 1990, The Classic Car Club of America, Del Plaines, Ill.

The Great Race Züst

The author wishes to thank Derek Marrable, Harvey Sharpe and David Burgess-Wise in England, Emmanuel Piat in France, Paul Kierstein in America and Donatella Biffignandi in Italy for their invaluable help in finding information.

Black-and-white photography courtesy of Centro di Documentazione, Museo dell'Auto, Turin, Italy.
Color photography by Cam Hutchins (www.carnut.ca).

Malmerspach

Ard op de Weegh of The Netherlands has a knack for uncovering rare barn finds in central Europe, as evidenced by this story. He has an eye for the legendary under the cryptic dust covering classics in forgotten garages and basements, and has contributed to a book titled *Sleeping Beauties* that was released in late 2008. The book was inspired by the article of the same name that appeared in *Automobile Quarterly*, Vol. 22, No. 2; a follow-up article on the hidden treasures appeared in Vol. 25, No. 2. Many thanks to Kay Hottendorff of Germany for facilitating the commission of this story on the Malmerspach cars via introduction to the author.

Photography by Arnoud op de Weegh.

Microcars

Sources used in preparation for this story include the following: In-person interview with LaShawn Hagler, assistant manager at the Bruce Weiner Microcar Museum; e-mail interview with Adam Quellin, author of *Microcars at Large!* published by Veloce Publishing, May 1, 2007; the August 1955 issue of *Mechanix Illustrated*; Bruce Weiner Microcar Museum web site at www.microcarmuseum.com; phone interview with Jim Janecek, editor of *The Vintage Microcar Club – Microcar News*, www.microcar.org.

Photography by the author.

Going Micro – Microtrucks

Special thanks to Mario Palma for allowing *AQ* access to his interesting array of the little "big" trucks, a number of which are rare. Thanks also to Tim Barden at Veloce Publishing in the U.K. for his help.

Photos courtesy of Veloce Publishing and Andrew Mort.

Coda

Special thanks to Liz Norris at JMPR Public Relations for sourcing information for this story on the Phantom Corsair. We attempted to present this experimental six-passenger coupe in its best light.

Photography courtesy JMPR.

Back Cover

Debossment of the Wayne badge from the *AQ* Photo and Research Archives.

Errata, Changes & Updates

In the Vol. 48 No. 2 Salon article featuring Hispano-Suiza, the following should be noted: driver Jean Chassagne's name was misspelled on p. 7; also on p. 7, the last paragraph in the left column should read: "These racing cars gave birth to the type Alfonso XIII, which by many is considered the first true sports car of the world. His Highness the King was very pleased to allow the marque to designate the new model after his name. The first Alfonso XIII was offered to him by the queen." In the "Race of Two Worlds" article in Vol. 48 No. 2, Fangio's middle name was misspelled on p. 78 – it is, in fact, Manuel. Two other missteps in this story: on p. 79, David Murray's name was incorrectly spelled "Murry"; on p. 80 Ecurie Ecosse was incorrectly identified as "Ecuri"; on p. 82, the name Sclavi should have been "Scalvia"; and on p. 84, Musso was not the winner of the '57 Mille Miglia; Piero Taruffi won in a Ferrari 315 Sport. The feature on the Simeone Collection in Vol. 48 No. 3, pp. 74-87, was incorrectly bylined. The author of this story was Pete Vack; our apologies to Pete for the credit omission.

Watercolor sketches by Don Getz

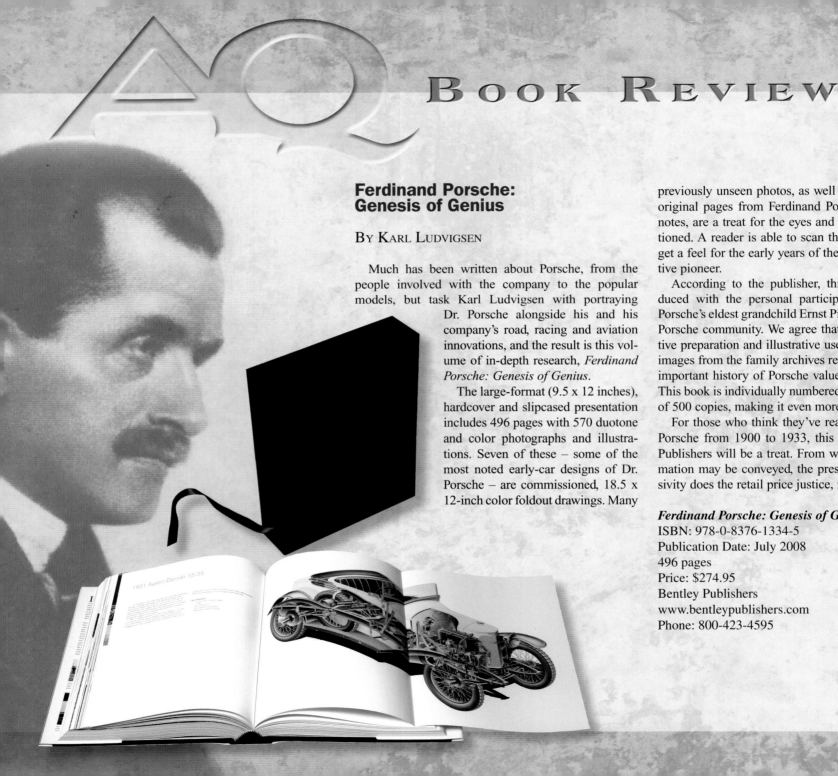

Ferdinand Porsche: Genesis of Genius

BY KARL LUDVIGSEN

Much has been written about Porsche, from the people involved with the company to the popular models, but task Karl Ludvigsen with portraying Dr. Porsche alongside his and his company's road, racing and aviation innovations, and the result is this volume of in-depth research, *Ferdinand Porsche: Genesis of Genius*.

The large-format (9.5 x 12 inches), hardcover and slipcased presentation includes 496 pages with 570 duotone and color photographs and illustrations. Seven of these – some of the most noted early-car designs of Dr. Porsche – are commissioned, 18.5 x 12-inch color foldout drawings. Many previously unseen photos, as well as reproductions of original pages from Ferdinand Porsche's handwritten notes, are a treat for the eyes and are adequately captioned. A reader is able to scan the images alone and get a feel for the early years of the legendary automotive pioneer.

According to the publisher, this edition was produced with the personal participation of Ferdinand Porsche's eldest grandchild Ernst Piëch as his gift to the Porsche community. We agree that the book's distinctive preparation and illustrative use of rare photos and images from the family archives reflect the quality and important history of Porsche values and philosophies. This book is individually numbered in a limited edition of 500 copies, making it even more exclusive.

For those who think they've read all there is about Porsche from 1900 to 1933, this book from Bentley Publishers will be a treat. From what little new information may be conveyed, the presentation and exclusivity does the retail price justice, if even more so.

Ferdinand Porsche: Genesis of Genius
ISBN: 978-0-8376-1334-5
Publication Date: July 2008
496 pages
Price: $274.95
Bentley Publishers
www.bentleypublishers.com
Phone: 800-423-4595

Micro Zeitgeist

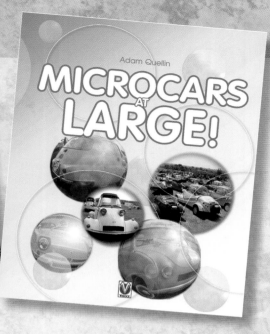

As was also illustrated in the two stories in this issue of *AQ* on microcars and microtrucks, two books produced by Veloce Publishing capture the essence of these unique and interesting vehicles. The simple charm and mechanical simplicity – for the most part – of these vehicles have made them significant collectibles over the past decade.

Micro Trucks
BY NORM MORT

The main takeaway from reading *Micro Trucks* by Norm Mort is that most, if not all, of the models discussed and photographed are unknown to most enthusiasts. That, in our opinion, is the most fascinating aspect to discovering production models from companies such as Autobianchi, Moto Guzzi, Vespa Ape and Diahatsu.

Novel models such as rare Iso utility vehicles are captured in detail in this 96-page book with 98 color photographs. According to Britain-based Veloce Publishing, this is the first book dedicated to microtrucks.

Actual production models and their complete specifications are presented, along with detail shots and restoration advice. For those who own these vehicles, author Norm Mort provides maintenance tips.

Micro Trucks
ISBN: 978-1-84584-175-1
Publication Date: July 2008
96 pages
Price: $29.95
Veloce Publishing
www.veloce.co.uk
Phone: 01305 260068

Microcars At Large
BY ADAM QUELLIN

Microcars have been admired by many for their place in motoring history. In *Microcars At Large*, this contribution to automotive history is aptly conveyed with concise prose by author Adam Quellin, who spells out the fact that these models originated in the immediate postwar period due to shortages of material and manufacturing facilities in Europe and Asia.

From there, evolution took over, creating consumer and business demand, thanks to clever innovation in design and engineering. Although noisy and small, microcars were the Model Ts for the impoverished regions.

Nicknamed "bubble cars," some models in this book are relatively well known in America, such as the Iso Isetta. Now collector's items, many enjoy cult status.

Full of color photography, this edition charts the history and development of microcars from the 1950s to the present day.

Microcars At Large
ISBN: 978-1-84584-092-1
Publication Date: February 2007
112 pages
Price $29.95
Veloce Publishing
www.veloce.co.uk
Phone: 01305 260068

Monstrosity and Marvel

I n the late 1930s, Rust Heinz of the H.J. Heinz family food empire sat down to design something totally different. The result was the Phantom Corsair, a one-of-a-kind and quite unique look at the future of automotive design. Maurice Bohman of famed coachbuilders Bohman & Schwartz helped Heinz create a vehicle labeled by some as both a "monstrosity and a marvel."

After the futuristic sharklike body was mated to a Cord 810 chassis, the Phantom Corsair's design evolved in a wind tunnel; its streamlined look gave it a distinct aerodynamic advantage, allowing it to reach speeds of 115 mph, impressive for a car its size in 1938. Many innovations were incorporated into the design, such as hydraulic impact bumpers, covered driving lights, climate control system and interior crash padding. Getting into the car may have been puzzling, as there are no door handles (the doors open via electric push buttons).

Bohman & Schwartz built the Phantom Corsair for an estimated $25,000. Heinz had plans to build a limited number for about $12,500 per car, but his untimely death shortly after its completion ended any production plans. After a stint at the 1939 World's Fair, it moved on to a new career in Hollywood as the mysteriously sinister "Flying Wombat" in the David O. Selznick production *The Young in Heart*, which starred screen legend Douglas Fairbanks Jr.

The vehicle was later sold to comedian Herb Shriner and was displayed for a time at the Silver Springs (Florida) Museum before ending up in the hands of collector William Harrah. Harrah had the car restored to its original configuration and displayed it as a showcase car in his vast collection.

Look for this unique car when it comes to the Amelia Island Concours d'Elegance, March 13-15, 2009, courtesy of the National Automobile Museum (The Harrah Collection).

"When this car came out of Bohman & Schwartz, people called it both outrageous and futuristic," said Bill Warner, founder and co-chairman of the Amelia Island concours. "It's a 70-year-old design that generates a buzz wherever it goes, and still defies description today, just as it did when it rolled out of their Pasadena shop in 1938. Voluptuous curves would seem out of place on such a hulking behemoth of a machine, but here they make sense."

ML

3/09